FOCUS on FITNESS

SECOND EDITION

NORTH CAROLINA STATE UNIVERSITY

Physical Education Department

KENDALL/HUNT PUBLISHING COMPANY
4050 Westmark Drive   Dubuque, Iowa 52002

Cover and chapter opener images
© Liquid Library (girl on treadmill)
© PhotoDisc (swimmer and tennis player)
© Photos.com (basketball player)

Printed in the United States of America
10 9 8 7 6 5 4

Contents

Preface

Welcome to Focus On Fitness. This text is designed to include fitness and wellness knowledge components as well as skill acquisition components that will assist you in becoming healthy and physically active. The textbook contains fundamental fitness and wellness knowledge that will supplement your class activities.

The text includes the five components of health-related physical fitness—cardiorespiratory, muscular strength, muscular endurance, flexibility and body composition—which have been identified as major contributors to wellness or disease prevention. Other areas, including nutrition, cancer, sexually transmitted diseases, stress management, cardiovascular wellness and fitness/sports related injuries.

The concept of wellness recognizes what each individual can do to enhance his or her health, based on self-responsibility for daily decision-making. On the wellness continuum, a premature death is at one end and a long-lived, high quality of life at the other. It is our daily choices about using tobacco, abusing alcohol, being physically active or sedentary, maintaining a well-balanced diet, wearing a seatbelt, or getting regular health screenings, and thinking and acting positively rather than negatively, which guide our movement toward one end of the continuum or the other. To a large degree, our health-related fitness and wellness are our own responsibilities.

Course learning outcomes: Students should be able to:

1. Demonstrate that they have learned the fundamentals of health-related fitness: cardiorespiratory and cardiovascular endurance, muscular strength and endurance, muscular flexibility and body composition.
2. Apply what they have learned about health-related fitness to meeting fitness goals established by the instructor and by students in their own training programs.
3. Demonstrate that they have acquired or enhanced skills, competencies, and strategies related to physical activities, such as aerobics, running, walking, and strength training.
4. Show that they possess a thorough working knowledge and appreciation of health-related fitness, including the importance of physical activity for a healthy life and an understanding of specific physical activities, as well as the role of health-related concepts such as nutrition, weight control and stress management.

Features

- Inquiry-guided learning: tenets of inquiry-guided learning will be interwoven throughout the text. This will provide students with the opportunity to collect data on themselves, analyze it, and draw conclusions concerning their own health-related fitness.
- End of chapter questions: there are questions for the students to answer at the end of each chapter to reinforce important material.
- Self-assessment activities: There are a variety of self-assessment worksheets and journals pertaining to health-related fitness in some chapters, as well as in the appendix for students.
- Support group organizations: There are several very helpful organizations listed at the end of some chapters for students to seek additional support.
- Internet web sites: Listed for the students are web site references at the end of each chapter.

Acknowledgments

We would like to thank the contributing authors in the Department of Physical Education at North Carolina State University and Dr. Louie Almekinders. Their knowledge, experience, time and research has made *Focus on Fitness* an invaluable, resourceful, contemporary text for students studying health-related fitness and wellness.

Dr. Louis Almekinders and Sally Almekinders,	Fitness/Sports Related Injuries
Darrin Dereu	
Joy Charles	Stress Management, Cancer
Kristine Clark	Editor, Cardiovascular Wellness,
	Nutrition, Appendix and Work Sheets
David Conner	Cardiovascular Wellness
Nita Horne	Cardiorespiratory Fitness, Work Sheets
	Inquiry-Guided Learning
Ted Jones	Photography
Dr. March Krotee	Preface
Marsha Lester	Flexibility
Dr. Kari Lewis	Adapted Physical Education
Chris Ousley	Sexually Transmitted Diseases
Paul Powers	Cancer
Ed Remen	Who's Your Doctor?
Ritchie Shufford	Wellness
Rex Smith	Body Composition
Heather Tatreau	Yoga
Arlene Tharrington	Core Conditioning
Dr. Debbie Williamson	Getting Started, Goal Setting
Tim Winslow	Editor, Muscular Strength and
	Endurance, Layout, Cover Design,
	Work Sheets, Preface, Appendix
George Youtt	Cardiovascular Wellness

Special thanks goes to Jessica Ward and Patrick Bedics for being the fitness models for the Muscular Strength and Endurance chapter. Also, special recognition goes to the North Carolina State University Athletics Department for the use of their Murphy Football Center's Strength Conditioning Facility. A special thanks to Brianne Racer, our Kendall/Hunt representative from start to finish.

Kristine Clark and Timothy Winslow, Department Editors

Congratulations on your new (or continued) commitment to physical fitness and wellness. A lifetime of fitness begins with the first step and we are pleased to assist you in reaching your goals. We believe that this textbook will be a valuable tool for you while you learn fitness guidelines and experience the physiological changes your body will make over the next several months.

Dr. T. C. Roberts, Department Head, Professor

SECTION 1

Goal Setting

Getting Started

Inquiries

1. Would you like to see a change in some area of your life (cardiovascular fitness, muscular strength, body shape, etc . . .) ? Explain what change(s) you would like to see.

_____

Responses of Others

_____

2. How soon would you like to see this change take place?

_____

Responses of Others

_____

3. What would be a long term goal that you would like to set for yourself to identify the specific change you want to see?

_____

Responses of Others

_____

4. What might be some of the short term goals that you would consider that would help you bring about this change?

_____

Responses of Others

_____

Goals motivate. Goal setting is a critical component of any exercise program. Knowing what you want to achieve can focus your time and attention on the necessary steps to take you where you want to go. Goal setting directs effort and gives one a sense of purpose. This can serve to motivate people who may otherwise lose interest in an activity or exercise program. Most people make statements that they would like to be in 'better shape' or 'lose weight' and become discouraged when they do not see results. Setting goals can help provide realistic expectations for change and keep one focused on the task providing the motivation to continue. Goal setting that results in improved performance does so because it directs attention to important elements of a skill, mobilizes efforts, encourages prolonged persistence and promotes the development of new learning strategies (Locke and Latham, 1985). In addition, goal setting is effective when certain conditions are met. Simply setting goals is not the answer. Goals must be well-planned, personal, written, realistic, short and long-term, measurable, time specific, monitored, and evaluated (Hoeger and Hoeger, 2000). Other keys to setting effective and appropriate goals follow.

Before goals are set, an individual must recognize which behaviors they want to change or maintain. Goals serve to facilitate growth toward a desired outcome and many times that outcome involves change. The decision to change behaviors and to maintain that change is positively impacted through the goal setting process.

Behavior Change

The need for goal setting is many times a result of a need to change certain behaviors or habits. Behavioral change progresses over time and through stages. Prochaska's Stages of Change (Prochaska, 1994) indicate that individuals proceed through six consistent stages of change. These stages of change are as follows:

Prochaska's Stages of Change

Precontemplation	Thinking about making a change, but decide it is too difficult and avoid doing it.
Contemplation	Have a desire to change but unsure how to go about making a change.
Preparation	Change appears to be possible and plans are made to make a change, this is likely a stage where goals are made.
Action	Have made and sustained change(s) for about six months.
Maintenance	Continue to practice new habits successfully for at least one year.
Termination	New habits have been established and efforts to change are complete.

Seven Key Steps to Effective Goal Setting

Locke and Latham (1990) propose a seven-step process to maximize the effectiveness of goal setting.

1. Set appropriate goals
   The first step in setting appropriate goals is to assess needs. Before goals can be set, one needs to know what the needs are. In addition, the function of the goal needs to be defined. Knowing the focus of the goal, the type of goal and the goal difficulty will aid in setting appropriate goals.
2. Develop goal commitment
   People need to be committed to goal achievement. Goal achievement can be enhanced when people participate in the goal setting process, when social support is provided and rewards for goal achievement are available.
3. Evaluate barriers to goal attainment
   Potential barriers to goal attainment need to be identified. Afterwards, strategies on how to overcome these barriers are necessary.

4. Construct an action plan.
   Setting goals without having a plan on how to implement them is a plan to fail. Goal setters must put an action plan in place for their goals to be effective. Knowing how to get to where you are going is critical. An action plan tells you how to get where you want to go.
5. Obtain feedback
   Feedback that contains information about how they are progressing toward goals is an important step to effective goal setting. Feedback can come from several sources. One possible source of feedback is the method of evaluation an individual chooses when goals are initially established.
6. Evaluate goal attainment
   Goal attainment and increased motivation is more likely when goals are periodically evaluated. A method of evaluation must be established when goals are set. There should be an organized method to evaluate where one is as they work toward their goals.
7. Reinforce goal achievement
   Goal setters are encouraged to repeat the goal setting process regardless of whether or not a goal was reached. Setting new goals enhances motivation and increases goal attainment.

Principles of Goal Setting

There are several goal-setting principles throughout the literature. The following principles are commonly found to be important components for a successful goal-setting program (Weinberg and Gould, 2003).

Set specific goals

To simply set out to "do-your-best" is not enough when change is necessary. Goals should be specific and measurable and stated in terms that are very well defined. Setting specific goals are most effective and easy to track and measure.

Set moderately difficult but realistic goals

Goals that are difficult to be challenging, but realistic enough to be achieved are the most effective goals. When goals are too difficult, frustration and a lack of confidence can result. On the other hand, goals that are very easily attained are generally of little value.

Set long-and short-term goals

Both long-term and short-term goals are important and must be set. In addition, short- and long-term goals must be linked to each other. Goals should progress logically according to predetermined objectives. Being able to meet short-term goals that lead to long-term goals can stimulate confidence and motivation.

Set performance and process, as well as outcome goals

Performance goals focus on achieving certain successes based on an individual's previous performance. With performance goals, one is more concerned with making comparisons with one's self and not with other people. Performance goals measure one's progress against one's self regardless of what others are doing or have done. Process goals, on the other hand, focus the attention on criteria that must be met during the performance so that performance goals can be met. Correctly executing an exercise (process goal) can result in the ability to lift more weight or run a longer distance (performance goal) thus winning a competition or race (outcome goal). Outcome goals focus on the result of an event and can create motivation to succeed on process and performance goals. However, too much focus on outcome goals can create anxiety.

Set practice and competition goals

When an individual chooses to compete, goals for practice and competition must be set. For most, more time is spent practicing for a competition and having specific goals for that practice time can help maintain motivation. Practice goals should compliment competition goals so that goals are more likely to be achieved.

Record goals

Goals should be recorded and posted. The method of recording is whatever one determines to be most practical. The purpose is to be reminded of set goals, regain focus on those goals and promote accountability.

Develop goal achievement strategies

Goal achievement strategies should indicate specifically how much, how often, how many, etc . . . The purpose of developing goal achievement strategies is to define specifically how a goal is to be achieved. This is similar to constructing the action plan mentioned above.

Consider the participant's personality and motivation

Knowing one's self will help determine how to set goals. For some, time restraints and schedules affect the method of how goals are to be achieved or maintained. Personality characteristics can also affect the structure and intensity of goal setting efforts.

Foster and individual's goal commitment

As mentioned earlier under the seven steps to effective goal setting, one must be committed to a goal before they can hope to achieve it. When people are allowed to set their own goals they take ownership in that goal and are more committed to it.

Provide goal support

Enlisting the support of significant others makes goal setting more effective. Educating those around you about your goals and the efforts you are making to achieve them can encourage support. This support is very important in progressing toward goals.

Provide evaluation of and feedback about goals

When goals are set there must be a method put in place to evaluate those goals. This is done at the start of the goal-setting process. Being able to adequately measure progress can provide feedback. This feedback must contain specific information relative to the progress, or lack thereof, in the effort to reach defined goals. Evaluation is critical and can provide the information needed to alter goals.

Common Problems in Goal Setting

The following are common problems often found in goal setting (Weinberg and Gould, 2003; Cox, 2007):

Poorly written goals

Goals should be written so they are specific, measurable, achievable, realistic and timely (SMART). When goals are vague, lack direction, cannot be measured and are unrealistic people are not motivated to strive to attain them. There is no motivation to attain goals that have no purpose or intent to change behavior. Writing goals in a specific manner will serve to motivate and facilitate change.

Setting too many goals too soon

People anxious to see change many times set too many goals too soon and become discouraged. A few realistic goals are better than several unrealistic goals. Having the time to realistically implement and monitor set goals is important to the effectiveness of goal setting.

Failure to devise a strategy

One of the goal setting principles above is to develop a goal setting strategy or action plan. The purpose of this strategy is to plan how one will achieve this goal. Not having a strategy or plan on how to achieve a goal results in certain failure for the goal setting process.

Failure to monitor progress

Knowing where one is in the process of attaining a goal is critical to not only achieving the goal, but also staying motivated to attain the goal. Well defined goals can be easily monitored. Having the ability to monitor progress will allow necessary adjustments to be made and will provide direction for future efforts.

Failing to adjust goals

Being aware of the possibility that goals may need to be adjusted can eliminate disappointment when changes need to be made.

Not planning for evaluation

When evaluation is planned for then one understands that periodic evaluation will occur and the effort to stay on task is encouraged. The lack of evaluation is a major reason for failure in goal setting programs. When there is no follow-up then there is no way to assess progress.

Steps to Designing a Goal-Setting System

The following are three basic steps to design a goal setting system:

Preparation and planning

Before setting goals one must assess abilities and needs. An integral part of assessment is identifying areas that need improvement or change. When needed changes are identified, a plan for how to achieve that change begins to take shape. Using the seven steps to effective goal setting and the principles of goal setting will provide direction on setting goals and formulating a plan to achieve them.

Set appropriate goals

As mentioned earlier, goals must be challenging but realistic. They must be well-planned, personal, written, realistic, short and long-term, measurable, time specific, monitored, and evaluated (Hoeger and Hoeger, 2000). What is appropriate for one person may not be appropriate for another. Setting the appropriate goals is the foundation for meeting those goals.

Evaluate goals

From the start, a plan on how to evaluate the goals you set must be established. When the goal is set, there should be an evaluation plan that corresponds to that goal. Knowing that there will be an evaluation motivates one to stay on task. Accurate evaluations provide necessary information so that one knows if and when to adjust goals along the way. More importantly, evaluating goals and progress toward a goal makes the probability of achieving that goal a reality.

Example of a specific goal, planned and written in a format that will allow for evaluation of success.

Long-Term Goal   I want to lose 10 pounds, measured by a body weight scale, in the next 2 months by doing 30 minutes of cardio a day, weight training 3x/wk, and following a healthy diet plan which I will monitor by using a goal chart.

Short-Term Goals	Week 1						
	Day 1	Day 2	Day 3	Day 4	Day 5	Day 6	Day 7
Cardio exercise for 30 minutes per day at 70% of THR							
Weight training a minimum of 3 days							
Eat 2300 calories or less per day							
Do not eat after 9 pm each day							
Drink 8 8oz.glasses of water per day							

A blank chart to write out your personal goal for the semester.

Long-Term Goal

Short-Term Goals	Week 1						
	Day 1	Day 2	Day 3	Day 4	Day 5	Day 6	Day 7

Review Questions

1. What is required to make a goal appropriate?
2. What stage of change are you in for your goal?
3. What are the seven steps to effective goal setting?

References

Hoeger, Werner, & Sharon A. Hoeger. (2000). *Lifetime Physical Fitness and Wellness,* Sixth Edition. Englewood, CO 80110: Morton Publishing Company.

Locke, E.A., & Latham, G.P. (1985). The application of goal setting to sports. *Journal of Sport Psychology, 7,* 205–222.

Locke, E.A., & Latham, G.P. (1990). *A theory of goal setting and task performance.* Englewood Cliffs, NJ: Prentice Hall.

Prochaska JO, Norcross JC, Clemente CC. *Changing for Good.* New York: William Morrow and Company, 1994.

Weinberg, Robert S. PhD., & Daniel Gould, PhD. (2003). *Foundation of Sport and Exercise Psychology.* Third Edition. P.O. Box 5076, Champaign, IL 61825-5076: Human Kinetics.

Websites

http://www.goal-setting-guide.com/smart-goals.html

http://www.dli.state.pa.us/landi/lib/landi/CWIA/2003_resource_guide/R-Goal_Setting.pdf Example Goal Setting Worksheet

http://www.educationoasis.com/curriculum/GO_pdf/goal_setting_worksheet.pdf Example Goal Setting Worksheet

SECTION 2

Health-Related Fitness
What Is Fitness?

Physical Fitness means that the various systems of the body are healthy and function efficiently so one can engage in activities of daily living, recreational pursuits and leisure activities without unreasonable fatigue.

Being physically fit is critical to our overall health and well-being. Physical fitness is directly associated with one's health. According to the American College of Sports Medicine, health-related fitness is divided into five components: 1) cardiorespiratory fitness, 2) muscular strength, 3) muscular endurance, 4) muscular flexibility and 5) body composition. These five components will be discussed in the next four chapters.

Physical Activity Pyramid

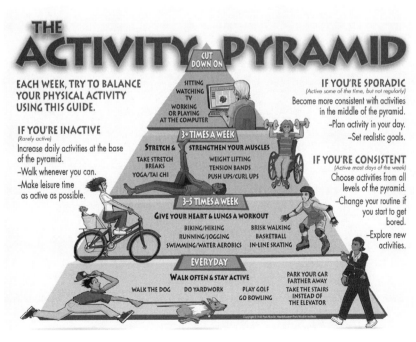

Copyright © 2003 Park Nicollet HealthSource, Minneapolis, U.S.A.

Cardiorespiratory Endurance

Inquiries

1. List some cardiorespiratory endurance activities you would like to do for this semester. What are some activities you would like to do in the future? Would you like to participate in any competitive events (i.e., road races, triathlons, cycling events)?

_____

_____

_____

Responses of Others

_____

_____

2. A good predictor of exercise adherence is previous sports or dance participation. What previous experiences have you had in these areas? What effect have they had on your current exercise patterns?

_____

_____

_____

Responses of Others

_____

_____

Cardiorespiratory Endurance

Cardiorespiratory endurance is the efficiency of the heart, lungs, and blood vessels working to meet the demands of prolonged physical activity by delivering adequate amounts of oxygen to the cells. As cardiorespiratory endurance improves, there is a decreased risk for heart disease.

Primary Functions of the Cardiorespiratory System

The Cardiorespiratory system is vital for our body to function. The main role of the cardiorespiratory system is to deliver nutrients and remove waste. The primary functions are listed below.

1. Transportation of oxygenated blood from the lungs to tissues and deoxygenated blood from the tissues to the lungs
2. Distribution of nutrients (glucose, free fatty acids, amino acids, etc.) to the body's cells
3. Removal of metabolic wastes (carbon dioxide, urea, lactate, etc.) from the periphery for elimination or reuse
4. Regulation of pH to control acidosis and alkalosis
5. Transportation of hormones and enzymes to regulate physiological function
6. Maintenance of fluid volume to prevent dehydration
7. Maintenance of body temperature by absorbing and redistributing heat   (Murray & Murray, 1998, p. 61)

Benefits of Improved Cardiorespiratory Endurance

There are many health-related and wellness benefits derived from improved cardiorespiratory endurance. These include both physiological and psychological benefits.

Physiological	Psychological

• Decreased fatigue in daily activities
• Improved work, recreational, and sports performance
• Decreased risk of
    Mortality from all causes
    Coronary artery disease
    Cancer (colon, breast)
    Hypertension
    Non-insulin dependent diabetes mellitus
    Osteoporosis
    Anxiety
    Depression
	• Improved blood lipid profile
	• Improved glucose tolerance and insulin sensitivity
	• Improved immune function
	• Improved body composition
	• Enhanced sense of well-being

(Holly & Shaffrath, 1998, p. 440)

Physiological Changes That Occur with Improved Cardiorespiratory Endurance

Positive changes that result with improved cardiorespiratory endurance can either be acute (short-term responses) or chronic (long-term/training responses). Acute changes can include a reduction in disease risk, improved energy level and improved sleep. Overtime, the chronic responses due to training result in a decreased resting heart rate, a decreased exercise heart rate at a given workload, increased heart size, improved strength of the heart muscle, increased stroke volume (amount of blood pumped per beat), increased total blood volume (potential 20–25% increase), and a two to three time increase in capillary density.

Resting Heart Rate

A true resting heart rate (RHR) is taken first thing in the morning for 60 seconds before rising from bed. After rising, the heart rate will increase possibly 10–20 beats per minute. If awakened by an alarm clock, the count can still be taken after resting quietly for several minutes. Resting heart rate will fluctuate for many reasons. These factors can include lack of sleep, medications, emotional stress, hydration level, food intake, caffeine, illness, environmental temperature, or humidity. Therefore, when determining your RHR, it is important to assess your resting heart rate on a number of mornings (at least 3–5) to determine an average RHR. Resting heart rate will vary greatly among individuals and is primarily dependent upon age and fitness level.

Check the table "YMCA Norms for Resting Heart Rate."

YMCA Norms for Resting Heart Rate (beats/min)

Age (yr)	18–25		26–35		36–45		46–55		56–65		>65	
Gender	M	F	M	F	M	F	M	F	M	F	M	F
Excellent	49–55	54–60	49–54	54–59	50–56	54–59	50–57	54–60	51–56	54–59	50–55	54–59
Good	57–61	61–65	57–61	60–64	60–62	62–64	59–63	61–65	59–61	61–64	58–61	60–64
Above average	63–65	66–69	62–65	66–68	64–66	66–69	64–67	66–69	64–67	67–69	62–65	66–68
Average	67–69	70–73	66–70	69–71	68–70	70–72	68–71	70–73	68–71	71–73	66–69	70–72
Below average	71–73	74–78	72–74	72–76	73–76	74–78	73–76	74–77	72–75	75–77	70–73	73–76
Poor	76–81	80–84	77–81	78–82	77–82	79–82	79–83	78–84	76–81	79–81	75–79	79–84
Very poor	84–95	86–100	84–94	84–94	86–96	84–92	85–97	85–96	84–94	85–96	83–98	88–96

Source: Adapted from: YMCA. Y's way to fitness. 3rd edition.

Assessing Cardiorespiratory Endurance

Cardiorespiratory endurance is assessed by monitoring the heart during activity. There are different methods that can be used to assess cardiorespiratory endurance. The most accurate method is called a stress test and is completed in a laboratory by trained exercise physiologist and/or physicians using sophisticated and expensive equipment. The test requires the individual to complete a specific treadmill or stationary bike protocol for as long as they can or until a specific endpoint. The heart is monitored with EKG electrodes on the chest and the individual must breathe through a mouth piece so the expired air can be collected for analyzing lung efficiency. An indirect and more practical method requires the exerciser to monitor their heart rate by assessing their pulse. Cardiorespiratory endurance can be assessed by this technique due to a linear relationship that exists between heart rate and oxygen uptake. An exerciser can count his/her own pulse by using the index and middle fingers of one hand (the thumb has its own pulse and should not be used) at an artery site. The most common sites for assessing pulse where arteries lie close to the surface of the skin are the radial artery (found on the wrist, thumb-side) and the carotid (found in the groove on the neck to the side of the trachea). The fingers should be pressed lightly at the site because pressing too hard may shut off the blood supply. The carotid artery has baroreceptors that will signal the brain to slow the heart rate if the fingers press too firmly, this could possibly result in the exerciser losing consciousness.

A simple, more accurate method for an individual to monitor their heart rate during exercise is to wear a heart rate monitor. Using a heart rate monitor provides real-time EKG accurate pulse readings. A chest belt that contains electrodes is placed high under the pectoral muscles by securing it with an adjustable strap. The electrodes detect the heart beat and transmit the signal to the wristwatch for the exerciser to view their heart rate. There is a three-foot transmission range for most monitors, so incorrect readings on the wrist watch can occur when someone else wearing a heart rate monitor gets too close. Heart rate monitors can be a very useful tool for competitors who train for racing or endurance events, as well as for recreational exercisers. The cost of a heart rate monitor varies from $40–$300 depending on the amount of functions it provides (stopwatch functions, setting of heart rate zones, recording splits, etc.).

Exercise Heart Rate

Assessing your exercise heart rate will depend on the type of activity you are doing and your exercise goals. Most exercisers take a heart rate count immediately post-exercise, but there are reasons to take the heart rate count at other times: pre-exercise, during exercise, immediately post-exercise and within a few minutes post-exercise. A pre-exercise count provides a relative base to compare the exercise heart rate. An unusually high pre-exercise heart rate may be due to one of the factors discussed previously for "fluctuations." During exercise the heart rate will plateau (rise during the warm-up and stay consistent through the aerobic phase, then drop during the cool-down); therefore, if the intensity remains the same, it will not matter when during the aerobic phase of the workout that the heart rate is counted. The post-exercise heart rate will be consistent with the aerobic phase heart rate, right before starting the cool-down. The recovery heart rate can be an indicator of fitness level. A fit individual will have a faster recovery in returning to the pre-exercise heart rate. Typically during an exercise class, heart rate will be monitored to determine if the exerciser is working at the appropriate intensity level.

Exercise heart rate needs to be counted within 15 seconds to prevent the heart rate from slowing down (due to decreased activity and decreased need for oxygenated blood to the working muscles) Therefore, the common amount of time to count the pulse for an exercise heart rate is 10 seconds. (Note: Some people prefer a 6-second count, because the exerciser only needs to add a "zero" to the count to have the beats per minute count. This is fine, but the concern is that if a beat or two is missed, it is then magnified by ten. For example, a 6-second heart rate count of 12 = 120 beats per minute. If one beat was missed, it actually should be 13 = 130 bpm or two missed beats, 14 = 140 bpm. This is a significant difference.)

Determining Your Target Heart Rate Zone for Exercise

Determining the appropriate target heart rate (THR) for exercise depends on an exerciser's resting heart rate, age, gender, and fitness level. The Karvonen Formula is preferred over the Maximum Heart Rate formula because it takes into account resting heart rate and gender. Rather than focus on a precise target heart rate (i.e., 140), a zone is calculated (i.e., 136–150). The purpose for achieving and staying within the THR zone is to maintain the appropriate intensity required for improvement of the cardiorespiratory system.

Predicted Baseline: Men = 220 Women = 226
Resting Heart Rate (RHR)
Predicted Maximum Heart Rate (PMHR)

(Women's hearts are smaller than men's and beat more times per minute.)

Here is the **Karvonen Formula** calculated for a **20-year old male, Beginner Fitness Level,** with a **Resting Heart Rate of 68 beats per minute.** Use the next page to calculate your Target Heart Rate Zone.

Baseline	220	Baseline	___	Baseline	___	Baseline	___	(baseline)
− Age	− 20	− Age	−	− Age	−	− Age	−	(minus age)
= PMHR	200	= PMHR	___	= PMHR	___	= PMHR	___	(= predicted maximum heart rate)
− RHR	− 68	− RHR	−	− RHR	−	− RHR	−	(− resting heart rate)
= HRR	132	= HRR	132	= HRR	___	= HRR	___	(= heart rate reserve)
× .60	× .60	× .70	× .70	× .80	× .80	× .90	× .90	(× intensity)
=	79.2	=	92.4	=	___	=	___	
+ RHR	+ 68	+ RHR	+ 68	+ RHR	+	+ RHR	+	(+ resting heart rate)
=	147.2	=	160.4	=	___	=	___	
10 sec ÷ 6		10 sec ÷ 6		10 sec ÷ 6		10 sec ÷ 6		(since 60 ÷ 6 = 10 sec)
=	24.5	=	26.7	=	___	=	___	(10-sec count)
	60%		70%		80%		90%	

Fitness Level: Beginner 60–70%   Intermediate 70–80%   Advanced 80–90%
Target Heart Rate Zone = 25 to 27 beats per 10 seconds
Note: For Swimming, MHR = 205. This is due to: non-weight bearing activity, horizontal body position, and cooling effect of the water.

Use this page to calculate your Target Heart Rate Zone.

Baseline: Men = 220 Women = 226
Resting Heart Rate (RHR)
Predicted Maximum Heart Rate (PMHR)

(Women's hearts are smaller than men's and beat more times per minute.)

Baseline	___	Baseline	___	Baseline	___	Baseline	___	(baseline)
− Age	−	− Age	−	− Age	−	− Age	−	(minus age)
= PMHR	___	= PMHR	___	= PMHR	___	= PMHR	___	(= predicted maximum heart rate)
− RHR	−	− RHR	−	− RHR	−	− RHR	−	(− resting heart rate)
= HRR	___	= HRR	___	= HRR	___	= HRR	___	(= heart rate reserve)
× .60	× .60	× .70	× .70	× .80	× .80	× .90	× .90	(× intensity)
=	___	=	___	=	___	=	___	
+ RHR	+	+ RHR	+	+ RHR	+	+ RHR	+	(+ resting heart rate)
=	___	=	___	=	___	=	___	
10 sec ÷ 6		10 sec ÷ 6		10 sec ÷ 6		10 sec ÷ 6		(since 60 ÷ 6 = 10 sec)
=	___	=	___	=	___	=	___	(10-sec count)
	60%		70%		80%		90%	

Fitness Level: Beginner 60–70%   Intermediate 70–80%   Advanced 80–90%
Target Heart Rate Zone = __ to __ beats per 10 seconds
or
Target Heart Rate Zone = __ to __ beats per 60 seconds

Exercise Prescription

Much like a drug prescription for an illness, exercise can be prescribed in varying dosages. The exercise dose, or quantity and intensity of exercise needed for the desired effect, will vary depending on the desired response (i.e., achieving high level of physical performance = high dose; lowering resting blood pressure = low dose). The interaction of the variables frequency, intensity, duration, and type of activity all determine the dose of exercise. This is called the FITT principle and is utilized to establish an individualized exercise prescription.

Exercise Prescription Guidelines	Health Benefits (i.e., blood pressure, cholesterol level)	Fitness Benefits (i.e., ↑ heart size, ↓ resting heart rate)
F requency: How often (days per week)	3 days per week	3–7 days per week
I ntensity: How hard (load/resistance)	Low to Moderate (40–60%)	Moderate to High (60–90%)
T ime: How long (length of training session)	20 minutes	≥20–60 minutes
T ype: Aerobic or Anaerobic Exercise	Aerobic Exercise	Aerobic Exercise

- **Aerobic Activities**—Use large muscle groups in a rhythmic, continuous manner, keeping heart rate consistently elevated for an extended period of time. The cardiovascular system is able to supply enough oxygen for activity to continue for long periods. Jogging, lap swimming, fitness walking, etc.
- **Anaerobic Activities**—Explosive, start-and-stop activities in which the heart rate fluctuates. Intensity is so great that the body is unable to deliver the oxygen that is demanded of the activity for it to continue for long periods. Weight training, sprinting activities, certain sports.

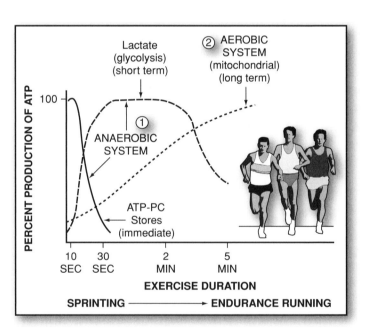

Figure 1.1 With an overlap of energy systems, the anaerobic system provides the working muscles with ATP from ATP-PC stores and the lactate or glycolysis path. The aerobic system provides ATP from mitochondria which require oxygen to burn carbohydrates and fats.

What Determines the Dose for an Exerciser?

The fitness level of the exerciser determines the dose.

	Beginner	Intermediate	Advanced
Frequency	3 days a week	3 to 5 days a week	5 to 7 days a week
Intensity	60–70%	70–80%	80–90% (see Karvonen Formula).
Time (minutes)	10–30	20–40	30–60
Type	Aerobic	Aerobic	Aerobic

Progression

The basis of all training programs is the principle of overload. When the current load (dose) is no longer a stressor, due to the body adapting to the demand, the load needs to be increased for further gains. An increase to one or more of the FITT principles can create an overload. (For example, the Beginner could choose a prescribed value from Intermediate to progress, until gradually the Beginner adapts all the FITT principles and becomes an Intermediate exerciser.). A beginning exerciser will want to stay at a low intensity during the first few weeks of training to prevent injuries.

Training Variations

It is important to have variety in your workouts to prevent boredom with exercise and to maintain an intensity level that will elicit continued training improvement. The training schedule could alternate hard and easy days rather than consist of a gradual progression. Within a single training session, the intensity could vary. Examples of intermittent activities in which intensity varies are: interval training, fartlek, and par course.

1. Interval training—Periods of relatively intense work are alternated with periods of active recovery. An example would be exercising at the high end of your THR zone (80–90%) for a short period, followed by an active recovery period at the low end of your THR zone (60–70%).
2. Fartlek (Swedish for "speed play")—A type of cross-country running involving jogging at varying speeds over varying terrain.
3. Par course—Combines continuous training with circuit training. Involves jogging a short distance from exercise station to exercise station, performing designated calisthenics at each station.

Components of a Cardiorespiratory Exercise Session

The three basic components of a cardiorespiratory exercise session are: warm-up, conditioning stimulus, and cool-down. The warm-up and cool-down may take between 5–15 minutes. This time frame will depend upon the age and fitness level of the exerciser (older individuals and those with increased risk of irregular heart events benefit from longer warm-up and cool-down periods). The warm-up represents a period of metabolic and cardiovascular adjustment from rest to exercise; the cool-down represents a period of metabolic and cardiovascular adjustment from exercise to rest. The most appropriate activities for the warm-up and cool-down are those that are similar to the conditioning stimulus, performed at 50% of the stimulus intensity. To increase flexibility, stretching activities may be appropriate in addition to the warm-up or cooldown activities.

Precautions for Participation in a Cardiorespiratory Endurance Program

Although participation is beneficial to almost everyone, physical limitations need to be identified first. Individuals over age 35 should complete a physical examination and receive clearance from their physician before participating in a fitness program, regardless of health status. Individuals having any medical problems should complete a physical examination and receive clearance from their physician, regardless of age. Overtraining should be avoided by progressing slowing and allowing the body time to recover between exercise sessions. It is important to cease exercising if pain is persistent. Terminate the exercise session and consult a physician if experiencing chest pain, dizziness, shortness of breath or nausea.

Record Keeping

Maintaining an activity log has many benefits and allows for personal reflection.Many serious exercisers report maintaining some kind of activity record. An activity record can be maintained by using a calendar, chart, log or a dairy format. An activity log can be found in Appendix F. An activity record allows an individual to set goals and monitor progress. The record can be a source of motivation or provide discipline to stick with the training program. The record can provide awareness of physical capabilities and physiological and psychological changes. An activity record can be useful tool in providing an early warning of overtraining which can lead to overuse injuries.

Review Questions

1. What is the purpose of determining your Target Heart Rate Zone?
2. As someone becomes more aerobically conditioned, will that individual's true resting heart rate lower (have less beats per minute) or increase (have more beats per minute)? Explain your answer.
3. During an activity that is aerobic, does the heart rate during the workout phase rise and fall continuously or plateau and remain elevated?
4. What factors might you vary to create an overload in your daily workout?

References

Brown, H.L. (1996). *Lifetime fitness.* Scottsdale, AZ: Gorsuch Scarisbrick, Publishers.

Corbin, C.B.; Lindsey, R.; Welk, G.J.; Corbin, W.B. (2002). *Concepts of fitness and wellness.* Boston: McGraw-Hill.

Holly, R.G. & Shaffrath, J.D. (1998). Cardiorespiratory endurance. In *ACSM's resource manual for guidelines for exercise testing and prescription* (pp. 437–447). Baltimore: Williams & Wilkins.

Howley, E.T. & Franks, B.D. (1997). *Health fitness instructor's handbook.* Champaign, IL: Human Kinetics.

McArdle, W.D.; Katch, F.I.; & Katch, V.L. (1996). *Exercise physiology.* Baltimore: Williams & Wilkins.

Murray, T.D. & Murray, J.M. (1998). Cardiovascular anatomy. In *ACSM's resource manual for guidelines for exercise testing and prescription* (pp. 437–447). Baltimore: Williams & Wilkins.

Nieman, D.C. (1995). *Fitness and sports medicine: A health-related approach.* Mountain View, CA: Mayfield Publishing Company.

Prentice, W.E. (2001). *Get fit, stay fit.* Boston: McGraw-Hill.

Web Sites for CardioRespiratory Fitness

http://acsm.org/ American College of Sports Medicine

http://www.cooperaerobics.com/default.aspx Cooper Aerobics Center

http://www.pe4life.com/ PE 4 Life

http://www.americanheart.org American Heart Association

http://www.strokeassociation.org/ American Stroke Association

http://www.fitness.gov/ The President's Council on Physical Fitness & Sports

http://www.cdc.gov/nccdphp/dnpa/physical/measuring/indes.htm Center for Disease Control Physical Fitness Intensity Guidelines

Muscular Strength and Endurance

Inquiries

1. List some options besides weight training, calisthenics, and sports to improve your muscular strength and endurance, and discuss the effectiveness of these options.

_____

_____

_____

Responses of Others

_____

_____

2. A friend has started taking performance-enhancing supplements to improve his lifting and muscle growth. What would you say or not say to your friend on this matter?

_____

_____

_____

Responses of Others

_____

_____

This chapter presents basic information regarding the development and maintenance of muscular fitness, muscular strength, and endurance. Although these three components of fitness can be developed using a variety of training methods or techniques, some form of weight training is probably the most efficient and popular method.

The benefits of weight training are discussed and important terms are defined. A simplified overview of the neuromuscular system and how it functions is presented. Basic guidelines are discussed, and finally, a description of weight lifting exercises and how to correctly perform them is provided.

A common question is, who will benefit from weight training? Because all movement is the result of muscle contractions, it can be safely argued that most everyone will benefit. Stronger muscles are able to function more efficiently and will make all movements easier to perform. The more sedentary you are, the more likely it is that your level of strength and endurance is low, and hence you would benefit more than a very active individual. Although the level of strength that is appropriate will vary between individuals, depending upon the demands of their occupations and their leisure time pursuits, everyone should develop and maintain a healthy level of strength and muscular endurance throughout their life.

The benefits of weight training are widely recognized by the health and medical communities, and weight training has become one of the most often prescribed forms of exercise. Listed below are some of the potential benefits of weight training:

- Improvement or maintenance of strength and endurance
- An increase in power
- Improvement or maintenance of bone density
- An increase in the strength of connective tissue (tendons and ligaments)
- An increase and/or maintenance of lean mass—improved body composition
- Helps maintain resting metabolism as we age, which is directly linked to lean body mass
- Improvement or maintenance of flexibility
- Improved posture
- Enhanced self-image
- Provides a healthy outlet for stress

With regards to lean body tissue, the old adage "use it or lose it" is certainly applicable. Our bodies are very adaptable and will quickly lose their strength and endurance if not subjected to a regular form of overload. Because few people have occupations or engage in leisure time pursuits that are physically demanding, it is very important from a fitness standpoint to incorporate strength training in their total exercise program.

Common Terms in Weight Training

- Strength—the maximum force that can be generated by a muscle or group of muscles for a single repetition. Strength is dependent upon many factors, including muscle size, muscle attachments, fiber type, and motor unit recruitment.
- Endurance—the ability of a muscle to generate force for an extended period of time. Strength and endurance, although related, can be thought of as being at opposite ends of a continuum, with each requiring very specific training
- Power—the ability to produce force rapidly. Work = force × distance and power = (force × distance) time. Power combines strength and speed, and is often the key factor in athletic success.
- Flexibility—the ability to move a joint through its full range of motion (ROM).
- Repetition (rep)—one complete movement of an exercise
- Set—some number of repetitions performed consecutively. The number of repetitions in a set is determined by the goals of the trainee.
- Atrophy—a loss of body tissue that is associated with disuse. All lean body tissue is subject to atrophy.

- Hypertrophy—an increase in muscle mass associated with exercise. Hypertrophy is controlled to some degree by the hormone testosterone, so males generally see a greater amount of hypertrophy than females with the same level of training.

Types of Progressive Resistance Training

- Isometrics—a form of exercise that employs pulling and pushing against immovable objects where there is no visible lengthening or shortening of the muscles
- Isotonics—a form of exercise characterized by exerting force against moveable objects such as barbells, dumbbells and the use of various machines where the muscles go through both concentric and eccentric actions. Due to the lever system formed from the muscles, bones and joints, the force generated will vary throughout the ROM. For example, with elbow flexion the biceps can produce maximal force when the elbow joint approaches 100 degrees but are relatively weaker at greater or lesser angles. For this reason, isotonics are subdivided into:
- Dynamic constant resistant exercises—the use of free weights (ie., barbells and dumbbells) where the resistance remains constant throughout the ROM
- Dynamic variable resistance exercises—the use of machines that employ a chain or belt that goes around an elliptically shaped cam that varies the resistance throughout the ROM. These machines are designed to match the resistance to the standard force curve for a given movement (ie., the ability of the user to produce force).
- Isokinetics—a form of exercise machine that controls the speed of movement and provides a varying resistance throughout the ROM. The resistance the user encounters exactly mirrors the force produced at a constant speed. These machines are expensive and are not usually available to most individuals.
- Plyometrics—a form of exercise that involves the rapid eccentric loading of a muscle, which activates the stretch reflex, thereby recruiting more motor units. This form of training was originally developed to improve jumping ability and to bridge the gap between strength and speed training. An example is repetitive jumping on and off boxes.

Types of Muscle Actions

- Isometric—this type of muscle action occurs when the muscle shortens, exerting a force that is equal to the resistance and neither lengthens or shortens.
- Concentric—this type of muscle action occurs when the muscle exerts a force that is greater than the resistance and shortens. For example, during the curl exercise, when the bar is curled from the straight arm position to the fully flexed position, the biceps is going through a concentric action.
- Eccentric—this type of muscle action occurs when the muscle exerts less force than the resistance and lengthens. Again, during the curl exercise, as the bar is lowered at a slow, controlled speed from the fully flexed position to the fully extended position, the biceps are going through an eccentric action. Weight trainers often refer to this type of training as negative reps. Interestingly, it has been determined that the delayed onset muscle soreness experienced after a workout is largely due to eccentric contractions.

Types of Weight Training

- General Weight Training—Many people are recognizing the impact that training with weights can have on strength, endurance, and body composition. Most general weight training programs borrow from the following groups.
- Olympic Weight Lifting—a form of competitive weight lifting in which the athletes perform two lifts—the clean and jerk, and the snatch. This form of weight lifting requires great strength, power, athletic ability and technique.
- Power Lifting—a form of competitive weight lifting in which the athletes perform three lifts—the bench press, the squat and the dead-lift. This form of lifting does not require the power and athletic

Weight Training Equipment

Free Weights	Weight Machines
• barbells are straight bars of varying length used for two handed exercises. An Olympic bar is seven feet long and weighs 45 pounds without collars. Dumbbells are used for one-handed exercises.	• of the many types and brands of weight machines, most are designed to provide dynamic variable resistance. For many people the safety and convenience of these machines make them the perfect choice.
Advantages:	*Advantages:*
1. more muscle is used (stabilization)	1. convenience (changing resistance is quick and easy)
2. greater range of motion	2. safety—no spotter is required
3. unlimited exercise choices so that muscles can be worked at various angles	3. Due to their design, many machines offer variable resistance throughout the ROM.
Disadvantages:	*Disadvantages:*
1. many exercises need a spotter	1. less muscle mass is used (no stabilization is required)
2. the resistance is constant	2. less variety of exercises and the ROM is fixed by the machine

ability of Olympic lifting. These three exercises develop many of the major muscle groups of the body and are used by both beginners and advanced weight trainers.

- Body Building—a form of competition where the participants are judged according to the size and symmetrical development of the entire musculature.
- Sports Training—Almost all athletes use some form of weight training to improve strength, endurance, and power and to lessen the chances of injury. Identifying the demands of the sport enables trainers to develop specific exercise programs to meet these demands.

Training Principle

- Overload—This principle states that in order for positive adaptations to take place (improved strength, endurance, etc.) the body must be subjected to greater stress (exercise is a form of stress) than that to which it is accustomed. Productive overloading involves the proper use of its four components: load, repetition, rest and frequency. The load or the intensity is the most important factor in strength development. Basically, strength is increased by lifting heavier weights and endurance is developed by performing more repetitions.
- Specificity—this principle states that how the body responds to exercise is dependent upon the type of stress and how the stress is applied. The adaptations that occur are very specific, so it is important to have goals and know how to train to reach these goals. The body builder and the Olympic weight lifter have different goals and therefore have very different training programs.
- Reversibility—often referred to as the "use it or lose it" principle, it states that any gains made through training will be lost with detraining. It has been determined, however, that the gains made can be maintained with less training than it took to achieve them.
- Individual Differences—this principle states that due to genetics, everyone's potential is different and progress will occur at different rates even when on identical training programs. Since few of us ever approach our genetic potential, we all can improve our fitness with proper training, good nutrition and adequate rest.

The Anatomy and Physiology of Movement

All human motion is the result of muscle contractions, and with training, the functional capacity of these muscles can be greatly improved. In order for a muscle to contract, two things are required—energy in the form of adenosine triphosphate (ATP) and a stimulus from the central nervous system. The arrangement of the bones of the skeletal system and how the muscles cross the various types of joints of the body determine the kinds of movement that are possible. For example: the elbow joint is a hinge joint that only allows for flexion and extension. The biceps and triceps cross the joint to the anterior and posterior respectively, and either flexion or extension will occur when they contract. A ball and socket joint like the hip is capable of many more movement patterns (flexion, extension, adduction, abduction and circumduction). The muscles that cross this joint do so from many angles, and the movement that results from their contraction is the direct result of how they cross the joint.

Muscle contractions are very complex processes that are initiated from the central nervous system in the form of an electrical stimulus. Due to their structure and the interaction of various chemical processes, muscle tissue has the unique ability to contract. A cross-sectional view of a whole skeletal muscle reveals that it is composed of thousands of individual muscle cells or fibers. Within each fiber are smaller threadlike strands called myofibrils that contain the actual protein filaments (actin and myosin) that enable the muscle fibers to contract. Movement occurs when the actin and myosin filaments slide past each other, shortening the fibers. All of the muscle fibers are grouped into bundles called fasciculi (muscle fiber bundles). Each individual fiber, the bundles of fibers and the entire muscle are all encased in layers of connective tissue. These layers of connective tissue ultimately tie into the tendons that attach to the bones of the skeletal system. Acting as a harness, the force generated in the muscle is transmitted via this connective tissue/tendon to the bone, resulting in movement. The arrangement of the fasciculi determines a muscles shape and is involved in its ability to generate force.

Each of the thousands of fibers in a muscle is stimulated by a nerve, a motor neuron. These motor neurons and the muscle fibers they activate are called motor units. The force of a muscle contraction depends in large part on how many fibers are in a motor unit and how many motor units are recruited. This selective recruitment gives us the control necessary to produce movements requiring gradations of force, from the very delicate and accurate to the very powerful and gross. Due to a natural level of inhibition we are unable, except perhaps in moments of extreme emotion, to recruit all the available motor units (a built-in safety feature). With training, however, we learn to recruit more motor units. Early strength gains experienced before muscle tissue has hypertrophied is mostly the result of the nervous system learning to recruit more motor units.

Muscle fibers (or more accurately motor units) are often classified according to their speed of contraction. Oversimplifying, the skeletal muscles fibers can be classified as either fast twitch or slow twitch.

Although muscles typically have a mixture of slow and fast twitch fibers, all of the fibers in a motor unit are of the same type. For slow movements or movements that require little force, slow twitch fibers are recruited, and for faster movements or movements requiring more force, slow and fast twitch fibers are recruited. Of special interest to the weight lifter is the fact that the body recruits muscle fibers in a set sequence, with slow fibers always the first to be recruited. Training with light resistance will not necessitate the recruitment and hence the development of fast twitch fibers. Due to their inherent qualities, fast twitch fibers have a greater capacity for anaerobic work (fast and intense) and slow twitch fibers have a greater capacity for aerobic work (endurance).

Research has shown that heredity largely determines the ratio of fast and slow twitch muscle fibers. With training, both slow and fast twitch fibers can take on some of the characteristics of the other fiber type, but conversion from one fiber type to the other does not seem to occur (at least not to any appreciable level).

Different Roles of Muscles

Skeletal muscles, which come in a wide variety of shapes, sizes and fiber composition, are responsible for every movement. During a movement in which they are involved they can function in different roles. They can act as:

- Agonists (prime movers)—when they are primarily responsible for a movement.
  EXAMPLE: the biceps brachii during elbow flexion and during the curl
- Antagonists—when they produce the opposite action of the prime movers
  EXAMPLE: the triceps brachii during elbow flexion and during the curl
- Synergists—when they assist the prime movers
  EXAMPLE: the brachioradialis during elbow flexion
- Stabilizers—when they help to stabilize the whole body or a particular body part
  EXAMPLE: the erectae spinae stabilizes the spine during the curl

Movements

The human body is capable of an infinite variety of movement. The fundamental movements are listed and defined below. These movements are defined from a standardized starting position (standing erect with the feet parallel and close together, with the arms away from the body with the palms facing forward), referred to as the anatomical position. More complex movements are variations and combinations of these fundamental movements.

- Flexion—a movement that results in decreasing the joint angle. For example, in elbow flexion the angle between the forearm and the upper arm is decreased.
- Extension—a movement that results in increasing the joint angle. In elbow extension, the angle between the forearm and the upper arm is increased.
- Adduction—movement toward the midline of the body. Moving the arm toward the side as in the end of a jumping jack exercise involves shoulder adduction.
- Abduction—movement away from the midline of the body. Moving the arm away from the body during the start of a jumping jack involves shoulder abduction.
- Rotation—movement that occurs around the vertical axis of the body or around the long axis of a limb. Shaking your head "no" involves rotation of the head. With regard to movement of the limbs, rotation is described as either internal or external rotation. Moving the front surface of the arm or leg away from the midline of the body is defined as external rotation and moving the front surface toward the midline is defined as internal rotation.
- Pronation—rotating the forearm so that the palm faces either down or backward. You would use a pronated grip when doing the pull-up exercise or reverse curl.
- Supination—rotating the forearm so that the palm faces forward or up—you would use a supinated grip when performing a curl.
- Plantar flexion—at the ankle joint when the toes are moved away from the shin (pointing the toes). Performing the heel raise exercise involves plantar flexion when you go up on the balls of the foot.
- Dorsi flexion—at the ankle joint when the toes are moved toward the shin.

Weight Training Guidelines

Every workout should begin with a warm-up. A typical warm-up includes about five minutes of whole body cardio type exercise to raise the heart rate, increase blood flow and increase muscle temperature. This is followed by easy whole body stretching and then a specific warm-up of the muscles to be used (usually a light set). Each exercise should be done through a complete range of motion in a slow, controlled fashion. Make sure to control the exercise through both the concentric and eccentric phase of the exercise. It is usually recommended that you take 1 to 2 seconds to perform the concentric phase and 2 to 3 seconds to perform the eccentric phase. It is important to avoid holding your breath during the execution of an exercise. The general rule is to breathe in during the eccentric phase (typically when lowering the weight) and breathe out during the concentric phase (typically when raising the weight). The first two to three weeks should be devoted to learning the correct technique and accustoming the body to the stress of lifting. Performing one set during the first week and gradually increasing the number of sets will aid in minimizing muscle soreness. Generally, allow 48 hours between weight training workouts for the same body part. A beginning program should consist of about 10 to 12 exercises that focus on the large muscle groups of the body. To insure symmetrical development, include at least one exercise for each of the large muscle groups.

American College of Sports Medicine Guidelines

For general muscular fitness, the American College of Sports Medicine recommends 1–3 sets of 8–12 repetitions 2–3 times a week. You should select multi-joint exercises that require the requirement of multi-muscle groups (bench press, overhead press, rowing exercises, squats, leg presses, etc.). Isolation exercises that involve a single joint and focus on less muscle mass should be used to complement your program. The program should be progressive and repeat itself periodically. Accomplish this by increasing the resistance in a systematic and regular fashion and by repeating the exercises on a regular basis. (Monday, Wednesday, Friday, for example). Incorporate variability into your program with respect to the exercises performed and the intensity at which they are performed. Learn a number of exercises for each large muscle group, and on different days, work at a different level of intensity. The FITT principle, frequency, intensity, time, and type of training, give shape to your program and will largely determine the level of improvement and success. The adaptations and improvement experienced will be specific to the frequency, intensity and volume of training—remember, training for general health and fitness requires much less effort than training for maximal sports performance. Selecting the amount of weight to use in training will be determined by your goals and is usually based on a percent of your 1 Rep Max (RM): the maximum weight that you can lift through a full ROM one time. Most research indicates that a load equal to about 75% of 1RM is necessary to promote strength gains. Most people can perform about 10 reps using 75% of their 1RM. Do not attempt a 1RM until you have mastered the lift and have been engaged in strength training for 4 to 6 weeks. The 1RM can be approximated by using the Brown formula: Maximum Weight = (Reps $\times$ .328 + .9849) $\times$ Resistance

The following chart will help in determining the resistance and the number of sets and reps to use in training for different goals:

TRAINING GOAL	RESISTANCE	# REPS	# SETS
Strength/power	Heavy	2 to 6	2 to 3
Endurance	Light	15 to 25	2 to 3
General conditioning	Medium	8 to 12	1 to 3

The amount of rest between sets is determined by your training goals, the system of training you are using and how much weight you are lifting. Training for strength and using a 2 to 6 RM/set in a priority system will require 2 to 3 minutes rest between sets. Super-setting will allow you to decrease this rest time.

Always perform the exercises that involve large muscle groups and are multi-joint type exercises first (bench press, overhead press, rowing exercises, squats, leg presses,etc). If single joint or small muscle group exercises are performed first, these small muscles will become the limiting factor rather than the large muscle groups you are trying to exercise. For instance, performing curls prior to pull-ups will pre-fatigue the biceps and make it difficult to adequately work the large, stronger muscles of the back.Although there are many systems for determining the number of sets and reps, the amount of resistance and order of exercise, most are variations of either the circuit training or the priority system. Circuit Training is a system of training where the individual performs single sets of a number of different exercises with a minimum amount of rest between exercises. The circuit can then be repeated until the desired number of sets for each exercise is met. This system is time efficient and is effective in developing muscular endurance and general conditioning and in maintaining a certain degree of fitness. Athletes often use circuit training during the season when maintenance is the primary goal and time is critical. Individuals primarily interested in strength development and more advanced weight trainers usually use a different system. Priority System is where an individual prioritizes the order of the exercises and performs a predetermined number of sets of each exercise before going to the next exercise. Some other common systems include super-setting, light-heavy, heavy-light and pyramid systems. Super-setting is a system of training in which exercises are paired. The individual performs a set of an exercise for one muscle group immediately followed by a set for a different muscle group. The paired exercises often work antagonistic muscle groups, or muscle groups from different areas of the body. For example, leg extensions and leg curls. The leg extension exercise works the quadriceps and the leg curl works the hamstrings, which are antagonistic muscle groups. Single or multiple sets of the paired exercises are performed before moving to the next pair of exercises. Since the muscle groups can recover while the other exercise is being performed, this system can greatly reduce the training time.

Safety is important at all times when lifting. The purpose of any physical training is to improve upon your present condition. Injuries due to poor form or lifting techniques can slow or stop your progress. The correct technique should be used to perform each exercise through the proper range of motion in a controlled fashion.

Correct technique includes maintaining proper body positioning and alignment, breathing and moving the joint through its full range of motion utilizing only the muscles that are appropriate. The spine is very strong when the normal curves are maintained in what is called neutral spine and therefore to protect the spine, lifts should be completed with a neutral spine. Spinal rotation and rounding the lower back during the execution of most exercises should be avoided. It is important to breathe through each repetition and therefore it is important to avoid holding your breathe during the lift. A spotter, someone to assist if the lift can not be completed, should be used when lifting weights above the body. Collars or clips should be used to keep the weight plates on the bar. Sliding plates can unbalance the bar and result in injury. Weight rooms are often busy and crowded. Be aware of what is going on around you and be prepared to protect your safety. Keeping a record of your training program that includes details of the weight, the number of sets and reps, and a brief descriptive analysis of the training session can be very valuable. To get the full benefits of weight training, progressive overload is necessary, by maintaining a record it is easy to insure appropriate weight increases occur. In addition to insuring progressive overload, record-keeping can be a motivational tool. It is important to realize that due to the principle of individual differences, everyone will progress at different rates even when on the same program. Your progress and success are going to be largely determined by the consistency and intensity of your training. Therefore, it is important to set realistic goals that result in the symmetrical development of all the major muscle groups of the body.

**Basic Weight Training Program
(Using Super Sets)**

EXERCISE

Bench Press
Seated Row

Overhead Press
Latpulldown/pullups

Curls
Tricep Extension

Squats
Back Extension

Leg Curls
Leg Extension

Heel Raises
Crunches

Perform each superset 1–3 times before proceeding to the next superset.

Exercises

Although there are virtually hundreds of different weight lifting exercises, most are variations of a relatively few. For instance the bench press can be performed on a flat bench, incline bench, decline bench, with barbells or dumbbells or using a machine. Listed below are some of the basic lifts that should be incorporated into most programs.

- Bench Press
  Prime Movers: pectorals, anterior deltoid, triceps
  Execution: Lie in a supine position on the bench with the feet flat on the floor. Grasp the bar with a pronated grip (palm away) and the hands a little wider than shoulder width. Slowly lower the bar until it touches the chest at the nipple line and then push the bar back to starting position. Do not bounce the bar off the chest or arch the back during the exercise.
  Variations: incline, decline, machine

- Overhead Press
  Prime Movers: deltoids, trapezius, triceps, upper pectoral, serratus anterior
  Execution: This exercise can be performed either standing or seated. Grasp the bar with a pronated grip with the hands slightly wider than shoulder width. With the bar at the upper chest position, press the barbell overhead until the arms are fully extended and then slowly lower to the starting position. Avoid leaning backward during the exercise and do not use the legs to assist in the movement.

- Lat-pulldown
  Prime Movers: latissimus dorsi, teres major, rhomboids, biceps
  Execution: Use a grip slightly wider than shoulder width with the palms facing away. Pull the bar down either in front of or behind your head to shoulder height. Keep your body in an erect position and avoid leaning back at the waist during the exercise. Using a narrow grip puts more emphasis on the biceps.

- Seated Row
  Prime Movers: rhomboids, latissimus dorsi, biceps
  Execution: This exercise is performed on a machine. Grasp the handles with an appropriate grip (many machines give options) and pull the arms straight back going through the full range of motion. Keep your chest against the pad and attempt to adduct the shoulder blades at the completion of the movement.

- Upright Row
  Prime Movers: trapezius, deltoids, biceps
  Execution: This exercise is performed in a standing position with the feet about shoulder width apart. The barbell is held against the front of the thighs with the arms fully extended, using a pronated grip. Keeping the bar close to the body, pull it up to the height of the clavicle. Avoid leaning forward to initiate the movement or backwards to complete the movement.

- Squats

  Prime Movers: gluteus maximus, quadriceps, hamstrings

  Execution: Squats are a multi-joint whole body exercise that work many stabilizing muscles in addition to the prime movers. They are one of the best overall exercises when done correctly. All beginners are recommended to have an instructor or experienced weight lifter assist them in learning the correct technique when first attempting this lift.

  With the barbell on the shoulders, stand with the feet about shoulder width apart, toes angled slightly outward. Slowly squat until the top of the thighs are parallel with the floor. Try not to let your knees go out over your toes. Keep your head up, eyes looking straight ahead or upwards, your torso nearly vertical and your back slightly arched. Do not round your back or allow the head to drop, as this will put tremendous stress upon your lower back. Maintain good body position, and without bouncing at the bottom, return to the starting position. Throughout the exercise, keep your feet flat on the floor—don't go up on the balls of the feet.

- Leg Press

  Prime Movers: gluteus maximus, quadriceps, hamstrings

  Execution: This exercise is performed on a leg press machine. Place your feet on the platform about shoulder width apart with your toes angled slightly outward. Lower the weight until the knees are at about a ninety-degree angle. Without bouncing at the bottom, push the weight back up to the starting position. Although the legs will be straight at the completion of the movement, avoid locking the knees.

- Leg Curl
  Prime Movers: hamstrings
  Execution: This exercise is normally performed on a special leg curl machine. Begin the exercise in a prone position with the padded bar across the back of your legs just above the ankles. Curl the moveable pad towards your buttocks by flexing your knees until it contacts the back of your legs. Slowly return to the starting position.

- Leg Extension
  Prime Movers: quadriceps
  Execution: This exercise is normally performed on a special leg extension machine. Adjust the machine so that the leading edge of the seat touches the back of your knees when you are sitting with your legs hanging straight down. The padded bar should be just above your ankles. Extend your knees until the legs are straight and then hold this position momentarily. Because of potential stresses in the knee joint, only lower the weight about 30 degrees. This is especially true if you are lifting heavy weights.

- Heel Raises
  Prime Movers: gastrocnemius, soleus
  Execution: This exercise is usually done a special machine but can be performed with a barbell or dumbbells. If you are in a standing position or where the legs are straight, both the gastrocnemius and the soleus are involved in the exercise. If you are in a seated position, only the soleus is involved—so the seated form of this exercise will seem harder. Keeping your legs extended (all movement should occur at the ankle joint), as you forcefully raise your heels as high as possible and then lower to the starting position.

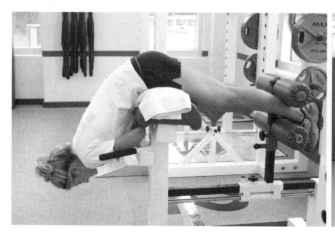

- Back Extensions
  Prime Movers: erector spinae, gluteus maximus
  Execution: This exercise can be most effectively and comfortably performed on a special apparatus. Start with your torso extending beyond the edge of the apparatus at 90 degrees with your lower body. Extend your trunk until your back is parallel with the floor—do not hyperextend—and then slowly return to the starting position.

- Curls
  Prime Movers: biceps brachii, brachialis, brachioradialis
  Execution: Stand erect with your feet about shoulder width apart and grasp the bar with a supinated grip. Your hands should be about shoulder width apart and your arms fully extended, so that the bar touches the front of your thighs. Keep your elbows stationary as the bar is curled (bar moves in an arc towards your shoulders) until your arms are fully flexed. Lower the bar to the starting position. Avoid leaning forward or backward to help curl the weight.

- Tricep Extension
  Prime Movers: triceps
  Execution: This exercise is performed on a machine or while lying on a bench in a supine position. The starting position when lying on a bench has you holding a D-Z curl bar with a pronated grip at arms length above your chest. Keeping your upper arms stationary, lower the bar until it lightly contacts the forehead. With movement only at the elbow joint, move the bar back to its starting position.

- Abdominal Exercises
  Prime Movers: rectus abdominus, obliques
  The muscles in the abdominal area perform a number of important functions. They flex and assist in rotating the trunk and support and contain the abdominal contents. Weak abdominal muscles have been identified as a contributing cause of low back pain. Some of the more common abdominal exercises include crunches, curl-ups, leg raises and side bends.
  The instructor will demonstrate the proper technique.

- Crunch—Palms Down

- Regular Push-Ups

- Modified Push-Ups

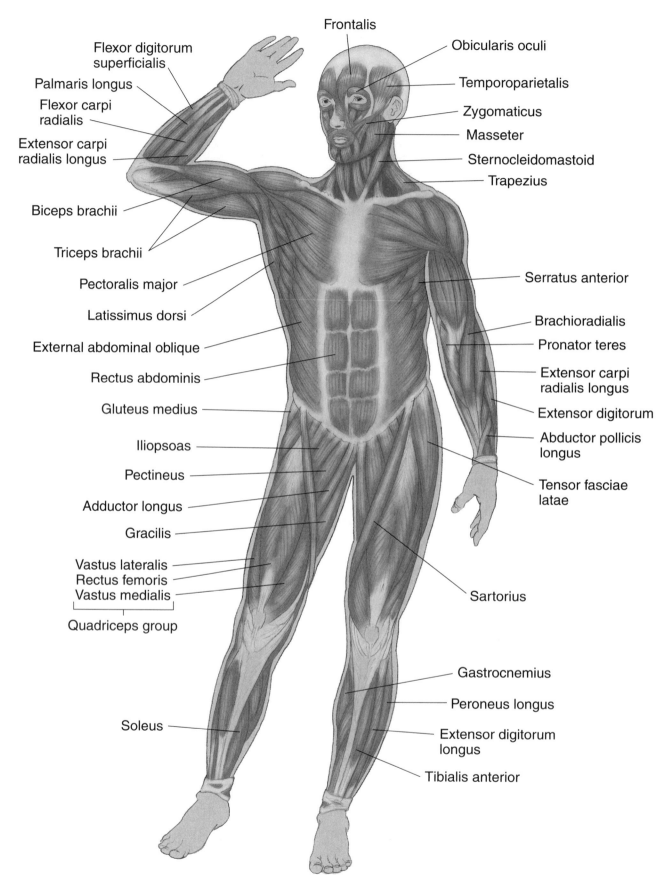

Figure 3.1   Human Skeleton (Anterior). Copyright © Kendall/Hunt Publishing Company.

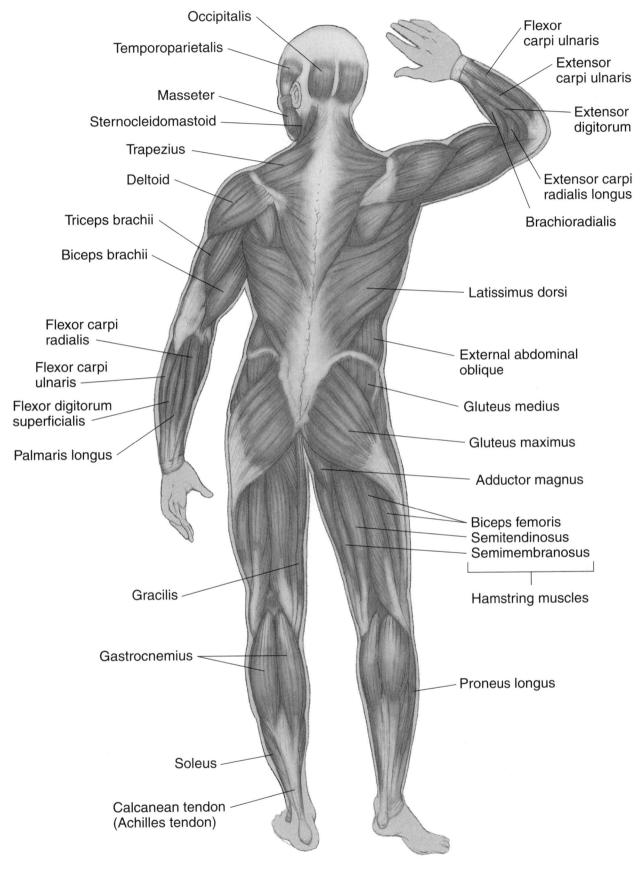

Figure 3.2   Human Skeleton (Posterior). Copyright © Kendall/Hunt Publishing Company.

Review Questions

1. A motor neuron and muscle fibers it activates is called a/an:
   a. Muscle fiber
   b. Motor unit
   c. Actin filament
   d. Power unit
2. When a muscle produces more force than resistance and shortens, this type of muscle action is called a/an:
   a. Eccentric action
   b. Isometric action
   c. Concentric action
   d. Fast twitch action
3. A type of progressive resistance training where the speed of movement is controlled and the resistance varies throughout the range of motion is called:
   a. Isometrics
   b. Isotonics
   c. Dynamic variable resistance
   d. Isokinetics

References

American College of Sports Medicine (2006). *ACSM's Guidelines for Exercise Testing and Prescription* (6th edition). Philadelphia: Lipincott/Williams & Wilkins.

Baechle, T. & Earle, R. (2001). *Essentials of Strength Training and Conditioning* (2nd edition) Champaign, Il: Human Kinetics.

Behnke, R. (2001). *Kinetic Anatomy* Champaign, Il: Human Kinetics.

Hesson, J. (2003). *Weight Training for Life* (6th edition) Wadsworth/Thomson.

Moran, G. & McGlynn (2001). *Dynamics of Strength Training and Conditioning* (3rd edition) New York: McGraw-Hill.

Web Sites

www.acsm.org American College of Sports Medicine
www.nsca-lift.org National Strength and Conditioning Association
www.nata.org National Athletic Training Association

Flexibility

Inquiries

1. Do you think stretching exercises are important? When should you perform stretching exercises?

   _____

   _____

   _____

   Responses of Others

   _____

   _____

2. Have you had any situation in which a flexibility program improved your health or well-being? Are there periods during your lifespan when a flexibility program might be more relevant?

   _____

   _____

   _____

   Responses of Others

   _____

   _____

Flexibility, Warm-Up, and Cool-Down Guidelines

Flexibility is defined as the ability to move a joint through its full range of motion (ROM). Stretching, the means by which we increase flexibility, is used as a part of an exercise workout to prevent muscular injuries, enhance performance, and aid in returning the body to its pre-exercise state.

Other potential benefits of increasing and maintaining a flexible body include:

- Increased production and retention of lubricants between connective tissue
- Reduction in the severity and frequency of muscular injuries
- Slows down the loss of joint mobility due to decline in flexibility experienced with aging
- Aids in developing and maintaining proper posture, thus reducing potential back pain
- Increased athletic performance
- May prevent, delay and/or lesson pain associated with arthritis
- Improvement in balance, stability, and coordination in the elderly for daily activities
- Reduction in stiffness, tightness and muscular tension
- Better neuromuscular coordination

The three basic methods of stretching are: static, dynamic, and proprioceptive neuromuscular facilitation (PNF). Static stretches are performed by slowly moving into an extended position, holding the position for a period of time, and then returning to a resting length. Dynamic stretching uses active movements to bring muscles through a full range of motion around the joint. This type of stretching is used as part of the warm-up. Proprioceptive neuromuscular facilitation (PNF) stretching consists of alternating isometric muscular contraction followed by passive stretching. There are various techniques that may be applied when performing this type of stretching. The most popular technique is a contract-relax-contract method. This method consists of elongating the muscle to be stretched, isometrically contracting the muscle for several seconds, relaxing the muscle, then immediately stretching the muscle using the antagonistic muscle, gravity or assistance. PNF stretching is the most effective method of increasing flexibility, but it is the most time-consuming and usually requires assistance.

As with the other components of fitness, we can use the acronym FITT to follow in developing and maintaining flexibility.

F: Frequency	2–5 times a week
I: Intensity	mild discomfort
T: Time	hold for 10–30 seconds
T: Type	static, dynamic, PNF

Exercise Warm-Up

The warm-up phase gradually prepares the individual's body for exercise. It takes the body from a resting state into one of vigorous activity. Increased muscle performance, movement performance, and injury prevention are the primary outcomes desired from the warm-up. Preparation for the warm-up should take into consideration the individual's age, physical limitations, capabilities, environmental conditions and the specific upcoming activity or workout.

Cardiorespiratory Warm-Up General Guidelines

The Cardiorespiratory warm-up should be at least five minutes in length. The speed of movement gradually increase from a slow to moderate pace and the movement around the joints being used should gradually increase. All movement should be smooth and rhythmic. Typically the warm-up is a low intense movement that is similar to the upcoming activity or workout.

Stretching Warm-Up General Guidelines

If stretching is done prior to beginning your workout, stretching should always follow the cardiorespiratory warm-up. Dynamic, static or a combination of both types of stretching can be used. If static stretching is used, it is best performed from a seated position in order to avoid stress on the low back. It is important to always breathe through the stretches and avoid holding the breathe. Each stretch should be performed slowly in a relaxed and controlled manner. Pain should never be felt when stretching. Avoid stretching that results in hyperextension, hyperflexion, unnecessary twisting of the joints, or extreme rotation (ie., backbends, straight-legged toe touches, hurdlers stretch, etc.). After the warm-up stretch is completed, similar to the cardiorespiratory warm-up, speed and movement around the joints should gradually be increased to ease into the workout.

Exercise Cool-Down

The cool-down phase of exercise is just as important as the warm-up phase. This part of the workout returns the body to its pre-activity resting state. The cool-down should be a complete reversal of the warm-up. The individual begins with a cardiorespiratory cool-down, followed by stretching the muscle groups used in the specific workout or activity.

An added benefit of stretching is increased flexibility. This is best accomplished when performed at the end of a workout or activity. At this time the muscles are warm and supple and circulation has increased, therefore these muscles are able to give maximum stretch.

If time permits, a final phase of relaxation techniques can be incorporated in the cool-down to aid in the total release of tension for the individual. These techniques consist of slow deep breathing exercises and combinations of muscle contractions, followed by relaxing individual muscle groups.

Cardiorespiratory Cool Down General Guidelines

A cardiorespiratory cool down should always be the first part of a cool down. This is typically a very low intensity movement of what the activity was. For example, if you ran for your activity, you will probably choose to cool down with a jog and/a walk. This allows for a gradual decrease in intensity allowing the heart to adjust properly. It should be about 3–5 minutes in length, long enough for the heart beat to return to baseline range and breathing to return to normal.

Effects of Warm-Up	Effects of Cool-Down
Increased heart rate	Aids in circulatory and metabolic exercise rates returning to normal levels
Increased blood flow, stroke volume, and oxygen exchange	Decreases muscle cramps
Increased muscle and blood temperature	Decreases muscle fatigue
Increased speed and strength of muscle contractions	Increases tendon, ligament, and muscle elasticity
Decreased muscle soreness, muscle/tendon strains and muscle/tendon tears	Decreases post-exercise muscle soreness
Increased range of motion	Decreases muscle stiffness
Increased muscle, tendon and ligament elasticity	Decreases risk of dizziness and fainting
Decreased muscle tension	Prevents a pooling of blood in the veins
Increased psychological preparedness	Aids in dispersement of latic acid
	Promotes relaxation of the mind and body
	Decreases body temperature

Stretching Cool-Down General Guidelines

Stretching should always follow the cardiorespiratory cool down once the heart rate and breathing have returned to pre-activity levels. Stretching should be done long enough to adequately stretch all the major muscle groups used in the activity. Static stretch is the most common method of stretching post-activity. With static stretching, each stretch should be held 10-30 seconds with 1-4 repetitions performed for each muscle. All stretches should be performed slowly in a relaxed and controlled manner. It is important to never force a stretch and to spend equal time on each side of the body. Always maintain continuous breathe throughout the stretches and avoid holding the breathe at any time. To maintain flexibility and to see improvements, stretching should be completed a minimum of 2 times a week and optimally at the end of each workout.

Assessing Flexibility

There is not one test that can test overall flexibility in an individual. Remember, the definition of flexibility is the ability to move a joint through its full range of motion. Therefore, each joint may have different levels of flexibility. A common test that is used to assess low back, hamstring flexibility is call the sit-and-reach test. This test is performed by sitting against a solid wall with the legs extended out in front of you and the feet resting against a box. The modified sit-and-reach test takes into account differences in arm and leg lengths. Sitting tall against the wall, arms should be extended with middle fingers stacked. The tester will then adjust the ruler to the tip of the fingers of the person being tested. Then the individual being tested will slide their fingers across the top of the ruler three different times with the best score taken.

Modified Sit-and-Reach

	Score at age				
	20–29	30–39	40–49	50–59	60+
Men					
High	>19	>18	>17	>16	>15
Average	13–18	12–17	11–16	10–15	9–14
Below Average	10–12	9–11	8–10	7–9	6–8
Low	<9	<8	<7	<6	<5
Women					
High	>22	>21	>20	>19	>18
Average	16–21	15–20	14–19	13–18	12–17
Below Average	13–15	12–14	11–13	10–12	9–11
Low	<12	<11	<10	<9	<8

Source: *ACSM Resource Manual for Guidelines for Exercise Testing and Prescription* (p. 165) by S. Blair, P. Painter, R. R. Pate, L. K. Smith, and C. B. Taylor, 1988, Philadelphia: Lea and Febiger. This was adapted from *The Y's Way to Physical Fitness* (pp. 106–111) by L. A. Golding, C.R. Myers, and W. E. Sinning (Eds.), 1982, Rosemont, IL: YMCA of the USA.

Review Questions

1. Flexibility is defined as the ability:
   a. Of muscles to be pliable in all their movements
   b. Of a joint to move freely through its full range of motion
   c. To perform movements without encountering resistance through motion
   d. Of groups of muscles to exhibit adequate mobility as they move joints through their respective planes of motion

2. To improve flexibility:
   a. Muscles need to be stretched beyond their normal range of motion
   b. Muscle elongation is required
   c. The intensity of mild discomfort must be reached
   d. All choices are correct
3. A warm-up consisting of both cardiorespiratory and stretching should last:
   a. 2 minutes
   b. 5 minutes
   c. 10 minutes
   d. 20 minutes
4. Increasing flexibility can be accomplished by all the following methods except:
   a. Static
   b. Progressive resistance
   c. Dynamic
   d. PNF

References

ACSM Fitness Book (3rd Edition), Human Kinetics, Champaign, Ill: 1998, ACSM.

Anderson B., & Anderson J. (2003). *Stretching, 20th Anniversary Ed.* Bolinas, California: Shelter Publications.

Caithersburg, M.D. (2001). *NIA, Exercise: A Guide From the National Institute on Aging.*

Fitness Stretching/Editions of Fitness Magazine with Karen Andes (2000). Three Rivers Press. New York, New York.

McAfkle, Katch; Katch; Lee and Febiger; (2000). *Essentials of Exercise Physiology,* 2nd Ed. Williams and Wilkins.

McAtee, (1999). *Facilitated Stretching,* Human Kinetics Publishing.

Moffat, Marilyn & Vickery Steve (1999). *The American Physical Therapy Association Book of Body Maintenance and Repair.* New York, New York: Round Stone Press, Henry Hold and Company, Inc.

Nieman, D.C. (2003). *Exercise Testing and Prescription: A Health Related Approach,* 5th Ed. New York: McGraw Hill.

Prentice, William E. (1999). *Fitness and Wellness for Life,* 6th Edition. McGraw-Hill.

Rankin, J.M. & Ingersoll C. (2001). *Athletic Training Management: Concepts and Applications,* 2nd Ed. McGraw-Hill.

Shier, J., Butler J. & Lewis R. (2003). *Hole's Essentials of Anatomy and Physiology,* 8th Ed. New York: McGraw Hill.

Web Sites

www.acsm.org American College of Sports Medicine
www.nia.nih.gov/exercise_book Exercise: A Guide From the National Institute on Aging
www.iFaFitness.com/stretch/index.html Stretch and Flexibility
www.gsu.edu/~wwwFit/Flexibility.html Georgia State University: Flexibility
www.physsportsmed.com The Physician and Sportsmedicine online

Body Composition

Inquiries

1. Are you content with your body size? From the illustration below, 1) mark which body you see yourself as presently and 2) mark which would be your ideal.

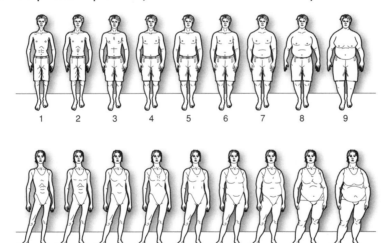

2. You notice a female friend who is practically starving herself in an attempt to become thinner. For the sake of her health you want to intervene. How might you do that in a successful way?

_____

_____

_____

Responses of Others

_____

_____

Introduction

Beginning at the age of 25, the average American male and female gain 1 pound of weight per year. So, by the age of 65, the average American will have gained some 40 pounds of weight. Due to the typical reduction of physical activity in our present day society, each year the average person also loses a half-pound of lean tissue. Therefore, this trend over a 40-year period has resulted in actual fat gain of 60 pounds, accompanied by a 20 pound loss of lean body mass. These gradual changes cannot be detected unless body composition is assessed periodically.

Body composition is considered to be the fat and notfat components of the body. The fat component of the human body is referred to as fat mass or percent body fat. The notfat component is usually referred to as lean body mass.

Essential and Nonessential Fat

The total amount of fat in the human body is classified into two basic categories: essential fat and nonessential fat (storage fats). Essential fat constitutes about 3% of the total weight in men and 12% in women. The fat percentages are higher in women due to gender-specific fat areas, such as the uterus, breast tissue and other gender-related fat deposits. Essential fat is stored in the marrow of bones, as well as in the heart, lungs, liver, spleen, kidneys, intestines, muscles and lipid-rich tissues of the central nervous system. This fat is required for normal physiologic functioning. It isn't quite clear whether this fat is expendable or serves as reserve storage. For females, an exceptionally low body fat percentage is especially of concern. Amenorrhea may occur at fat levels of less than 10% and 11–16% for many women. National standards indicate that males should not possess less than 5% body fat and females less than 10%. Storage fat, or nonessential fat, is the other category which consists of fat that accumulates in excess amounts so that over-fatness or even obesity can occur. Just as the percentage of body fat should not drop too low, it should not get too high either. There is a desirable range of fatness that is associated with good metabolic fitness, good health and wellness.

Body Mass Index

Body mass index (BMI) is another technique scientists and physicians use to determine thinness and excessive fatness. This is done by dividing the weight in kilograms by the square of the height in meters, or multiplying your weight in pounds by 705 and dividing the figure by the square of the height in inches. According to the BMI scale, the lowest risk for chronic disease is in the 22 to 25 range. Individuals are classified as overweight between 25 and 30. BMIs above 30 are defined as obesity and below 20 as underweight.

To calculate BMI

$$BMI = \frac{weight\ (kg)}{Height\ (m)^2}$$

or

$$BMI = \frac{weight\ (lb)\ x\ 704.5}{Height\ (in)^2}$$

Assessing Body Fatness

Body composition is considered to be the relative amount of fat and lean body mass. The normal range for women is 20–25 percent and 12–20 percent for men. When the body fat exceeds 30 percent for women and or 20 percent for men, the risk of chronic disease rises drastically. There are several methods used in assessing body fatness, but there are some advantages and disadvantages associated with each method.

Hydrostatic weighing was once considered the leading standard of body composition analysis. Hydrostatic measurements are based on the assumption that the density and specific gravity of lean tissue is greater than that of fat tissue. Thus, lean tissue will sink in water and fat tissue will float. However, there are several limitations to the hydrostatic weighing method. The equipment required to perform hydrostatic measurements is bulky and maintenance intense. The total test procedure may require 45 minutes to one hour. A large 100-gallon tank of water must be maintained at a constant temperature.

The most accurate method is DEXA (dual-energy x-ray absorptiometry scan). This is a relative new technique that originally was developed to measure bone density. However, researchers today use it to analyze body composition by determining the differentiation among bone, other lean tissue and fat.

Plethysmography uses air displacement, done by using a device called a Bodpod. When using this technique, a person sits in a sealed chamber of known volume and displaces a certain volume of air.

Bioelectrical impedance analysis (BIA) measures the rate at which a small amount of electric current flows through the body between electrodes placed on the wrist and ankle. Fat tissue does not conduct electricity as well as lean tissue; it resists or impedes the current. Electrolytes containing fluids, such as fluid found

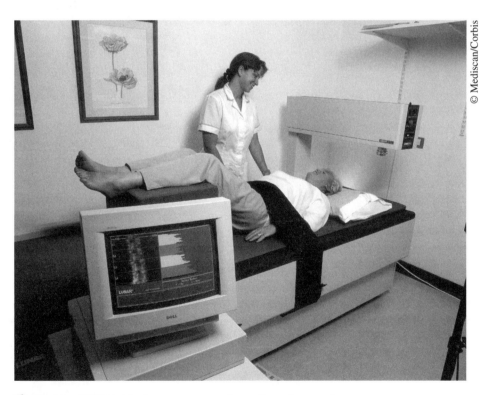

© Mediscan/Corbis

Figure 4.1   DEXA (dual-energy x-ray absorptiometry scan).

Figure 4.2   BodPod. Photo courtesy of Life Measurement, Inc., Concord, CA

mostly in lean body tissues, is less likely to cause resistance. The impedance reading allows the researcher to calculate total body water and then estimates total lean body mass and body fatness.

A common method of assessing fatness is the use of a caliper device to measure the thickness of substantial fat stores. The skinfold measurements are considered to be the more practical method of assessing body fatness. By measuring skin fold thickness at several sites around the body, it is possible to estimate total body fatness. Skinfold measurements are often used more frequently because they are less complicated and not nearly as costly. The more sites that are measured on the body, the more accurate the body fatness estimate will be. However, measurements of two or three skinfolds have been shown to be reasonably accurate and be administered in relatively short time.

- Tricep fold: one-half the distance between the tip of the shoulder and the tip of the elbow
- Iliac crest skinfold: top front of the iliac crest
- Thigh skinfold: front of the thigh midway between the hip and the knee
- Chest skinfold: to the right of the right nipple (one-half the distance from the midline of the side and the nipple)
- Abdominal skinfold: one inch to the right of the navel

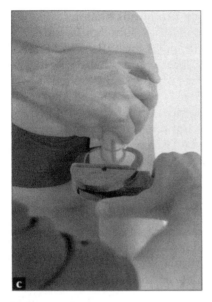
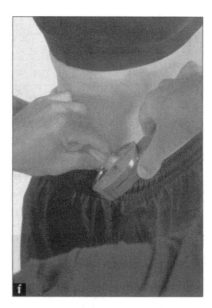

Figure 4.3   Skinfold locations for women. From the National Strength and Conditioning Association, edited by T.R. Baechle and R.W. Earle, 2004 *NSCA's Essentials of Personal Training*. Copyright © 1994 by the National Strength and Conditioning Association. Reprinted with permission from Human Kinetics (Champaign, IL).

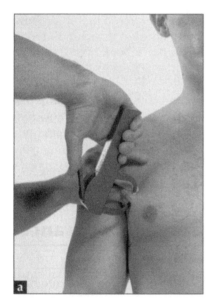
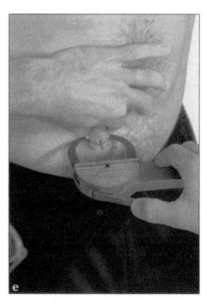
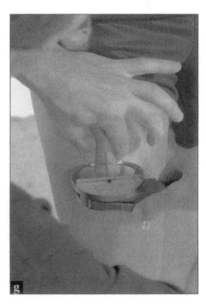

Figure 4.4   Skinfold locations for men. From the National Strength and Conditioning Association, edited by T.R. Baechle and R.W. Earle, 2004 *NSCA's Essentials of Personal Training*. Copyright © 1994 by the National Strength and Conditioning Association. Reprinted with permission from Human Kinetics (Champaign, IL).

Percent Fat Estimates for Women, Calculated from Triceps, Suprailium, and Thigh Skinfold Thickness

Sum of 3 Skinfolds	Age								
	23 Under 22	28 to 27	33 to 32	38 to 37	43 to 42	48 to 47	53 to 52	to 57	Over 58
23– 25	9.7	9.9	10.2	10.4	10.7	10.9	11.2	11.4	11.7
26– 28	11.0	11.2	11.5	11.7	12.0	12.3	12.5	12.7	13.0
29– 31	12.3	12.5	12.8	13.0	13.3	13.5	13.8	14.0	14.3
32– 34	13.6	13.8	14.0	14.3	14.5	14.8	15.0	15.3	15.5
35– 37	14.8	15.0	15.3	15.5	15.8	16.0	16.3	16.5	16.8
38– 40	16.0	16.3	16.5	16.7	17.0	17.2	17.5	17.7	18.0
41– 43	17.2	17.4	17.7	17.9	18.2	18.4	18.7	18.9	19.2
44– 46	18.3	18.6	18.8	19.1	19.3	19.6	19.8	20.1	20.3
47– 49	19.5	19.7	20.0	20.2	20.5	20.7	21.0	21.2	21.5
50– 52	20.6	20.8	21.1	21.3	21.6	21.8	22.1	22.3	22.6
53– 55	21.7	21.9	22.1	22.4	22.6	22.9	23.1	23.4	23.6
56– 58	22.7	23.0	23.2	23.4	23.7	23.9	24.2	24.4	24.7
59– 61	23.7	24.0	24.2	24.5	24.7	25.0	25.2	25.5	25.7
62– 64	24.7	25.0	25.2	25.5	25.7	26.0	26.2	26.4	26.7
65– 67	25.7	25.9	26.2	26.4	26.7	26.9	27.2	27.4	27.7
68– 70	26.6	26.9	27.1	27.4	27.6	27.9	28.1	28.4	28.6
71– 73	27.5	27.8	28.0	28.3	28.5	28.8	29.0	29.3	29.5
74– 76	28.4	28.7	28.9	29.2	29.4	29.7	29.9	30.2	30.4
77– 79	29.3	29.5	29.8	30.0	30.3	30.5	30.8	31.0	31.3
80– 82	30.1	30.4	30.6	30.9	31.1	31.4	31.6	31.9	32.1
83– 85	30.9	31.2	31.4	31.7	31.9	32.2	32.4	32.7	32.9
86– 88	31.7	32.0	32.2	32.5	32.7	32.9	33.2	33.4	33.7
89– 91	32.5	32.7	33.0	33.2	33.5	33.7	33.9	34.2	34.4
92– 94	33.2	33.4	33.7	33.9	34.2	34.4	34.7	34.9	35.2
95– 97	33.9	34.1	34.4	34.6	34.9	35.1	35.4	35.6	35.9
98–100	34.6	34.8	35.1	35.3	35.5	35.8	36.0	36.3	36.5
101–103	35.2	35.4	35.7	35.9	36.2	36.4	36.7	36.9	37.2
104–106	35.8	36.1	36.3	36.6	36.8	37.1	37.3	37.5	37.8
107–109	36.4	36.7	36.9	37.1	37.4	37.6	37.9	38.1	38.4
110–112	37.0	37.2	37.5	37.7	38.0	38.2	38.5	38.7	38.9
113–115	37.5	37.8	38.0	38.2	38.5	38.7	39.0	39.2	39.5
116–118	38.0	38.3	38.5	38.8	39.0	39.3	39.5	39.7	40.0
119–121	38.5	38.7	39.0	39.2	39.5	39.7	40.0	40.2	40.5
122–124	39.0	39.2	39.4	39.7	39.9	40.2	40.4	40.7	40.9
125–127	39.4	39.6	39.9	40.1	40.4	40.6	40.9	41.1	41.4
128–130	39.8	40.0	40.3	40.5	40.8	41.0	41.3	41.5	41.8

Body density is calculated based on the generalized equation for predicting body density of women developed by A.S. Jackson, M.L. Pollock, and A. Ward, reported in *Medicine and Science in Sports and Exercise,* 12 (1980), 175–182. Percent body fat is determined from the calculated body density using the Siri formula.

Percent Fat Estimates for Men Under Age 40 Calculated from Chest, Abdomen, and Thigh Skinfold Thickness

Sum of 3 Skinfolds	Age							
	Under 19	20 to 22	23 to 25	26 to 28	29 to 31	32 to 34	35 to 37	38 to 40
8– 10	.9	1.3	1.6	2.0	2.3	2.7	3.0	3.3
11– 13	1.9	2.3	2.6	3.0	3.3	3.7	4.0	4.3
14– 16	2.9	3.3	3.6	3.9	4.3	4.6	5.0	5.3
17– 19	3.9	4.2	4.6	4.9	5.3	5.6	6.0	6.3
20– 22	4.8	5.2	5.5	5.9	6.2	6.6	6.9	7.3
23– 25	5.8	6.2	6.5	6.8	7.2	7.5	7.9	8.2
26– 28	6.8	7.1	7.5	7.8	8.1	8.5	8.8	9.2
29– 31	7.7	8.0	8.4	8.7	9.1	9.4	9.8	10.1
32– 34	8.6	9.0	9.3	9.7	10.0	10.4	10.7	11.1
35– 37	9.5	9.9	10.2	10.6	10.9	11.3	11.6	12.0
38– 40	10.5	10.8	11.2	11.5	11.8	12.2	12.5	12.9
41– 43	11.4	11.7	12.1	12.4	12.7	13.1	13.4	13.8
44– 46	12.2	12.6	12.9	13.3	13.6	14.0	14.3	14.7
47– 49	13.1	13.5	13.8	14.2	14.5	14.9	15.2	15.5
50– 52	14.0	14.3	14.7	15.0	15.4	15.7	16.1	16.4
53– 55	14.8	15.2	15.5	15.9	16.2	16.6	16.9	17.3
56– 58	15.7	16.0	16.4	16.7	17.1	17.4	17.8	18.1
59– 61	16.5	16.9	17.2	17.6	17.9	18.3	18.6	19.0
62– 64	17.4	17.7	18.1	18.4	18.8	19.1	19.4	19.8
65– 67	18.2	18.5	18.9	19.2	19.6	19.9	20.3	20.6
68– 70	19.0	19.3	19.7	20.0	20.4	20.7	21.1	21.4
71– 73	19.8	20.1	20.5	20.8	21.2	21.5	21.9	22.2
74– 76	20.6	20.9	21.3	21.6	22.0	22.2	22.7	23.0
77– 79	21.4	21.7	22.1	22.4	22.8	23.1	23.4	23.8
80– 82	22.1	22.5	22.8	23.2	23.5	23.9	24.2	24.6
83– 85	22.9	23.2	23.6	23.9	24.3	24.6	25.0	25.3
86– 88	23.6	24.0	24.3	24.7	25.0	25.4	25.7	26.1
89– 91	24.4	24.7	25.1	25.4	25.8	26.1	26.5	26.8
92– 94	25.1	25.5	25.8	26.2	26.5	26.9	27.2	27.5
95– 97	25.8	26.2	26.5	26.9	27.2	27.6	27.9	28.3
98–100	26.6	26.9	27.3	27.6	27.9	28.3	28.6	29.0
101–103	27.3	27.6	28.0	28.3	28.6	29.0	29.3	29.7
104–106	27.9	28.3	28.6	29.0	29.3	29.7	30.0	30.4
107–109	28.6	29.0	29.3	29.7	30.0	30.4	30.7	31.1
110–112	29.3	29.6	30.0	30.3	30.7	31.0	31.4	31.7
113–115	30.0	30.3	30.7	31.0	31.3	31.7	32.0	32.4
116–118	30.6	31.0	31.3	31.6	32.0	32.3	32.7	33.0
119–121	31.3	31.6	32.0	32.3	32.6	33.0	33.3	33.7
122–124	31.9	32.2	32.6	32.9	33.3	33.6	34.0	34.3
125–127	32.5	32.9	33.2	33.5	33.9	34.2	34.6	34.9
128–130	33.1	33.5	33.8	34.2	34.5	34.9	35.2	35.5

Body density is calculated based on the generalized equation for predicting body density of men developed by A.S. Jackson and M.L. Pollock, *British Journal of Nutrition,* 40 (1978), 497–504. Percent body fat is determined from the calculated body density using the Siri formula.

Criterion Scores and Normative Values for Percent Body Fat for Males and Females

Male rating (criterion scores)	Age (years)						
	6–17**	18–25	26–35	36–45	46–55	56–65	66+
Very lean	<5 (not recommended)	4–7	8–12	10–14	12–16	15–18	15–18
Lean (low)	5–10	8–10	13–15	16–18	18–20	19–21	19–21
Leaner than average	—	11–13	16–18	19–21	21–23	22–24	22–23
Average (mid)	11–25	14–16	19–21	22–24	24–25	24–26	24–25
Fatter than average	—	18–20	22–24	25–26	26–28	26–28	25–27
Fat (upper)	26–31	22–26	25–28	27–29	29–31	29–31	28–30
Overfat (obesity)	>31	28–37	30–37	30–38	32–38	32–38	31–38

Male percentiles (normative references)***	20–29	30–39	40–49	50–59	60+
90	7.1	11.3	13.6	15.3	15.3
80	9.4	13.9	16.3	17.9	18.4
70	11.8	15.9	18.1	19.8	20.3
60	14.1	17.5	19.6	21.3	22.0
50	15.9	19.0	21.1	22.7	23.5
40	17.4	20.5	22.5	24.1	25.0
30	19.5	22.3	24.1	25.7	26.7
20	22.4	24.2	26.4	27.5	28.5
10	25.9	27.3	28.9	30.3	31.2

Female rating (criterion scores)*	6–17**	18–25	26–35	36–45	46–55	56–65	66+
Very lean	<12 (not recommended)	13–17	13–18	15–19	18–22	18–23	16–18
Lean (low)	12–15	18–20	19–21	20–23	23–25	24–26	22–25
Leaner than average	—	21–23	22–23	24–26	26–28	28–30	27–29
Average (mid)	16–30	24–25	24–26	27–29	29–31	31–33	30–32
Fatter than average	—	26–28	27–30	30–32	32–34	34–36	33–35
Fat (upper)	31–36	29–31	31–35	33–36	36–38	36–38	36–38
Overfat (obesity)	>36	33–43	36–48	39–48	40–49	39–46	39–40

Female percentiles (normative references)***	20–29	30–39	40–49	50–59	60+
90	14.5	15.5	18.5	21.6	21.1
80	17.1	18.0	21.3	25.0	25.1
70	19.0	20.0	23.5	26.6	27.5
60	20.6	21.6	24.9	28.5	29.3
50	22.1	23.1	26.4	30.1	30.9
40	23.7	24.9	28.1	31.6	32.5
30	25.4	27.0	30.1	33.5	34.3
20	27.7	29.3	32.1	35.6	36.6
10	32.1	32.8	35.0	37.9	39.3

When person trainers assess a client's body composition, they must account for a standard error of the estimate (SEE) and report a range of percentages that the client falls into.Note that the minimum SEE for population-specific skinfold equations is ±3–5%. Therefore, if a 25-year-old male client's body fat is measured at 24%, there is a minimum of a 6% range (21%–27%) that suggests a criterion-reference score of "fat." Note that reporting a client's body fat percentage with an SEE range can also cover any gaps and overlaps in the criterion-referenced norms shown. For example, what is the criterion score for a 30-year-old male with 29% body fat? The minimum SEE of ±3% places this client between 26% and 32% and therefore would suggest a criterion-reference score of "fat-overfat" or "borderline overfat."

*Data for male and female rating (criterion score), ages 18–66+, are adapted from Morrow, Jackson, Disch, and Mood 2000.

**Data for male and female rating (criterion score), ages 6–17, are from Lohman, Houtkooper, Going 1997.

***Data for male and female percentiles (normative references) are reprinted from ACSM 2000.

Adapted from Golding, Myers, and Sinning 1989.

From the National Strength and Conditioning Association, 2004, NSCA's Essentials of *Personal Training,* ed. T.R. Baechle and R.W. Earle, pages 246–247, table 11.14. © 2004 by the National Strength and Conditioning Association. Reprinted with permission, from Human Kinetics (Champaign, IL). Adapted from L.A. Golding, C.R. Myers and W.E. Sinning, 1989, Y's Way to Physical Fitness, 2nd ed, p. 125–136.

Review Questions

1. The method of determining body composition that involves sending a very low level of electrical current through a persons body is:
   a. Bod Pod
   b. Bioelectrical Impedance Analysis
   c. Skinfold Measurement
   d. Underwater Weighing Method
2. Why is knowing your Body Mass Index (BMI) so important?
3. The name of a machine that uses air displacement to measure body composition is:
   a. Near Infared Reactance
   b. Bod Pod
   c. Bioelectrican Impedance
   d. Skinfold Calipers

References

American College of Sports Medicine, (2003). *ACSM Fitness Books,* 3rd Ed. Human Kinetics.

Baechle, T. & Earle, R. (2004). *Essentials of Strength Training and Conditioning.* Champaign, IL: Human Kinetics.

Dykema, R. 2005, *Yoga For Fitness and Wellness,* Thompson/Wadsworth Publisher.

Hoeger, S.A. & Hoeger W.K. (2005). *Fitness and Wellness* 6th Ed. Thomson and Wadsworth.

Insel, P.; Ross, D.; & Turner R. (2004). *Nutrition,* 2nd Ed. Jones and Bartlett Publishers.

Satchidanada, S. 1979, *Integral Hatha Yoga,* Integral Yoga Publication.

Web Sites

www.acsm.org American College of Sports Medicine
www.brianmac.demo.co.uk.fat.htm
www.bioanalogics.com/brtech.htm
www.topendsports.com/testing/bodycomp.htm

Section 3

WELLNESS

Wellness reflects how one feels about life as well as one's ability to function effectively. Wellness is an expanded idea of health. It is the ability to live life fully, with vitality and meaning. True wellness is determined by the decisions you make about how to live your life. There are seven interrelated dimensions of wellness. The strength of each of these dimensions will vary at different stages in an individual's life. All must be developed in order to achieve wellness. The following wellness topics will be discussed in the next seven chapters: nutrition, cardiovascular wellness, stress management, fitness/sports related injuries, cancer, addictive behaviors, and sexually transmitted infections.

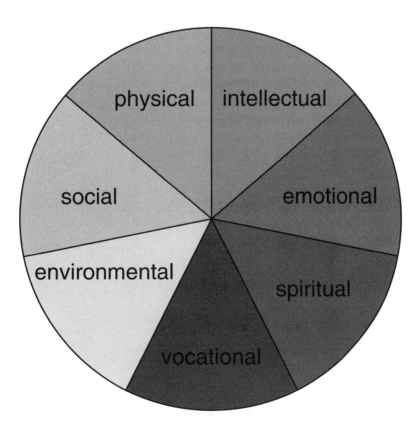

Seven Dimensions of Wellness

Physical Dimension—Keeping your body functioning at its maximum capacity over the entire lifespan.

Intellectual Dimension—Embracing lifetime learning.

Emotional Dimension—Experiencing and expressing a wide range of feelings and coping with life's occurrences.

Spiritual Dimension—Reflecting upon what inspires and motivates each individual intrinsically.

Vocational Dimension—Identifying and using skills, abilities and interests to incorporate into your life's work.

Environmental Dimension—Acknowledging the interdependence between man and earth and other living beings.

Social Dimension—Being able to create and sustain relationships with family, friends, peers and acquaintances over time.

Lifestyle Management

An individual makes healthy decisions through either enhancing wellness or reducing risks. For lifestyle management, an internal focus of control is an advantage. If an individual has an internal focus of control, they know that the source of responsibility for the events in one's life is oneself, instead of forces outside of their control. The choices you make can have a direct impact in prevention of the leading causes of death (heart disease, cancer, stroke, accidents, etc.) in the United States.

Examples of Lifestyle Management That Contribute to Wellness.

1. Being Physically Active
2. Eating a Healthy Diet
3. Maintaining A Healthy Body Weight
4. Managing Stress Effectively
5. Avoiding the Use of Tobacco and reduce or eliminate alcohol
6. Protecting Yourself from Disease and Injury
7. Using Medical Assistance When Necessary
8. Recycling
9. Using Morals and Ethics in Everyday Decisions
10. Building Healthy Relationships
11. Learning New Things
12. Balancing Work & Social Life

Nutrition

Inquiries

1. Describe your eating habits. Is there anything you would change?

_____

_____

_____

Responses of Others

_____

_____

2. Do you think that you only eat when you are hungry? What other purposes might food and eating be serving in your life?

_____

_____

_____

Responses of Others

_____

_____

We live in a society where food is over-consumed and individuals are physically inactive. The majority of our food choices are high in calories, sugar, fat, especially saturated fat and low in essential nutrients. As a result Americans have become heavier. Obesity has been declared a national epidemic with over 60% of the population overweight and obese.

A healthy diet should include food items high in nutrient quality that can provide energy and the substances needed for tissue growth, repair and maintenance. To help you understand how this can be accomplished, this section will address the six essential nutrients, MyPyramid, how to read food labels and the dietary guidelines from the Department of Agriculture and Health and Human Services and the Institute of Medicine. This chapter will also briefly address weight management.

Six Essential Nutrients

Nutrients can be classified into six categories based on their structure and the functions they perform in the body. These categories are carbohydrates, proteins, fats, vitamins, minerals and water. Of these six nutrients, only three provide energy. You can calculate your daily energy needs by using the chart in Appendix E. The other three are important in metabolic processes, tissue growth, repair and maintenance.

Carbohydrates

Carbohydrates are the main fuel source for the body, especially during exercise, and the only fuel source for the brain. Carbohydrates provide 4 kilocalories per gram. Carbohydrates also have a role in the metabolism of fat. When carbohydrates are limited, there is an incomplete breakdown of fat, resulting in the buildup of ketones, an acid byproduct.

Carbohydrates are classified by their structure and can be divided into three groups. Monosaccharides are the simplest carbohydrate unit. They are the "simple" sugars such as glucose, fructose and galactose. Disaccharides are two monosaccharides linked together. Common examples are the "simple" sugars sucrose, maltose and lactose. Polysaccharides are large chains of monosaccharides linked together. They are "complex" sugars such as starch and fiber. Fiber is an element in carbohydrates that is difficult or impossible for humans to digest. The daily recommended amount is 20–35 grams of fiber. Good sources include fresh fruits and vegetable as well as foods made from whole grains.

When carbohydrates are ingested, insulin is released into the blood stream. Some carbohydrates cause an immediate spike in blood insulin while others result in a slower insulin release. The effect carbohydrates have on the speed of insulin released into the blood stream is known as the glycemic index. High glycemic index foods include simple sugars, white rice, and potatoes. Low glycemic index foods include whole grains and fiber rich foods.

The recommended intake of carbohydrates should be between 40–50% of total calories. This is about 300 g/day for a person who weights 154 pounds. A very active individual or athlete should increase carbohydrate intake to 60% or 400–600 g of their total daily calorie intake.

Protein

Amino acids are the basic unit or building block for protein. There are 20 different amino acids of which 8 (nine in children and stressed older adults) are "essential" amino acids that must be obtained through the ingestion of foods. The remaining 12 are considered nonessential because they can be manufactured by the body. Individuals who are considered vegetarians must consider these parameters when selecting daily food choices.

Proteins are important for tissue growth and repair. Proteins also regulate the acid-base quality of body fluids. Proteins provide 4 kilocalories per gram. However, they are an inefficient fuel source.

Proteins are classified as complete or incomplete. Complete protein sources provide all the essential amino acids. Incomplete proteins lack one or more of the essential amino acids. Eggs are a perfect protein, to which all other food sources are compared. In addition, meat, dairy products and soy are complete proteins. Incomplete proteins include whole grains, legumes, and rice.

The recommended daily intake of protein for adults is 0.8 g per 2.2 kg of body weight. To find out how much protein you require, divide your body weight by 2.2 and multiply by .8. Example: (140 divided by 2.2) × .8 = 50.9 g protein. (Protein needs can also be calculated by simply multiplying .36 g per pound of body weight). The average individual should get 10–15% of daily caloric intake from protein.

Fats

Fats are also an important energy source for our bodies, especially during low intensity exercise and while we are resting. Fat is a dense fuel source, providing 9 kilocalories per gram. In addition to being an energy source, fats have other important functions in the body. One, fat provides cushioning and protection for our body's vital organs. Two, fat stores also function as insulation, allowing our bodies to retain heat. Three, fats are important for the transport of the fat-soluble vitamins, A, D, E and K. In addition, from dietary fat we obtain essential fatty acids that are important for making needed compounds in the body. Finally, fats provide foods with texture and flavor, and help us to feel satiated after a meal.

Of the three types of fats common in foods, (triglycerides, phospholipids, and sterols) triglycerides make up about 95% of the fat we eat. Triglycerides are also the form of fat commonly found in the body. Triglycerides can be classified by their length, level of saturation and shape. Fatty acids are designated as either short, medium- or long-chain depending on the number of carbon atoms in the chain. Chain length determines how the fatty acids are digested and absorbed by the body. The major digestion of fats occur in the small intestine.

The designation of saturation is based on the number of double bonds in the fatty acid chain. Saturated fats have no double bonds, therefore they can be packed more tightly, which is why most saturated fats are solid at room temperature. The unsaturated fats, monounsaturated and polyunsaturated, contain one or more than one double bond in the chain and are typically in the cis shape, therefore, these fats tend to be liquid at room temperature because they cannot be packed tightly together.

Another form of fat that occurs naturally, but is prominent in our food due to a man-made process, is trans fat. Trans fats are made by heating unsaturated fats to remove some or all of the double bonds, resulting in a chain similar or close to that of saturated fat. Trans fats are used especially in processed crackers and snacks in order to prolong shelf-life. If you read hydrogenated or partially hydrogenated oil in the list of ingredients, the product contains trans fat. Because trans fats are as great a concern as saturated fats, food manufacturers are now required to list the amount of trans fat in their products. Trans fats, like saturated fats, increase LDL levels and decrease HDL levels, contributing to the onset of heart disease.

Sources of Tryglycerides

Type of fat	Food sources
Saturated	Animal sources: cheese, whole milk, half and half, lard, bacon, hot dogs
	Tropical oils: palm oil, coconut oil
Monounsaturated	Olive, peanut, canola and avocado oils
Polyunsaturated	Corn, safflower, sunflower, soybean, sesame and vegetable oils
Trans fat	Processed foods: snack crackers, cookies, cereals

Cholesterol is a sterol type of fat found in foods of animal origin or synthesized within the body. Cholesterol is not found in vegetable food sources and is negligible in egg whites and skim milk. The highest content of cholesterol is found in egg yolks. Other foods that contain large amounts are red meat, organ meats (liver, kidney, and brain) and dairy products such as ice cream, butter, cheese and whole milk.

In the body, we are typically concerned about High Density Lipoproteins (HDL) and Low Density Lipoprotein (LDL). HDL is produced in the liver and small intestine and is known as the "good" cholesterol because it protects against heart disease by removing cholesterol from the artery wall and carrying it to the liver, where it is converted into bile and excreted through the intestine.

LDL is known as the "bad" cholesterol because it deposits cholesterol on the artery walls which can build up, resulting in plaque formation, which causes limited or stopped blood flow.

In the United States our dietary fat intake on average is about 40–50% of our total caloric intake. The American Heart Association suggests a diet of less than 30% of total calories from fat, with saturated, mono-unsaturated, and polyunsaturated fats making up 10% each. Cholesterol is continually manufactured by the body and should be limited to less than 300 mg per day.

Vitamins

Vitamins are water-soluble or fat-soluble organic substances required in small amounts to regulate important processes in the body and to perform very specific functions for the metabolism of carbohydrates, fats and proteins for energy.

The fat-soluble vitamins, A, D, E and K, are stored in the liver and fat cells of adipose tissue and are retained for a relatively long time in the tissue. Daily consumption of these vitamins is unnecessary and could result in toxicity. They are absorbed with dietary fat in the intestines.

Fat-Soluble Vitamins

	Function	Sources
Vitamin A	Important in vision and resistance to infection	Leafy green vegetables, yellow and orange vegetables, milk, butter, cheese
Vitamin D	Growth of bones and calcium absorption	Eggs, dairy products, fortified milk, fish liver oil
Vitamin E	Antioxidant* to prevent cell damage by free radicals	Seeds, leafy green vegetables, margarine
Vitamin K	Blood clotting	Green leafy vegetables, cereals

Antioxidants are compounds such as vitamins C, E, beta-carotene and the mineral selenium, which prevent oxygen from combining with other substances so that it may cause damage, thought to play a role in preventing heart disease and cancer.

Water-soluble vitamins, B vitamins and vitamin C, dissolve in water and are associated with the water parts of food and body tissue. Water-soluble vitamins are absorbed through the intestinal wall directly into the bloodstream. Water-soluble vitamins cannot be stored in the body and, if not used, will be flushed out in the urine. Your diet must contain these on a regular basis.

Water-Soluble Vitamins

Vitamin	Function	Sources
Thiamine (B1)	Releases energy from carbohydrates during metabolism; growth and muscle tone	Fortified cereals and oatmeal, rice, pasta, meats, whole grains and liver
Riboflavin (B3)	Releases energy from protein, fat and carbohydrates during metabolism	Whole grains, green leafy vegetables, organ meats, milk and cheese
Pyridoxine (B6)	Builds body tissue and aids in metabolism of protein	Fish poultry, lean meats, bananas, dried beans, whole grains, avocado
Cobalamin (B12)	All development and functioning of the nervous system; protein and fat metabolism	Meats, milk products and seafood
Folate (folic acid)	Genetic material development and red blood cell production	Green leafy vegetables, organ meats, dried peas, beans and lentils
Niacin	Carbohydrate, fat and protein metabolism	Meat, poultry, fish, potatoes, dairy products, eggs, enriched cereals
Vitamin C (ascorbic acid)	Bone, cartilage, muscle and blood vessel structure; maintains capillaries and gums; aids in absorption of iron	Citrus fruit, berries, vegetables—especially peppers

Minerals

Minerals differ from the other essential nutrients in that they are not broken down during digestion or absorption–they maintain their structure in all environments. Minerals have many functions in the body. One, they help maintain proper fluid balance and normal cell and muscle activity. Two, they provide structure in the formation of bones and teeth. Three, they help maintain normal heart rhythm, muscle contractions and nervous conduction. Four, they regulate metabolism.

Our bodies can't make minerals, so we must get them through our food. There are 18 minerals known to be useful to the body and 7 are considered essential and have FDA requirements. Minerals are divided into two groups, major and trace, based on how much is found in our bodies and how much we need to consume through our diet.

Major Minerals: greater than 100 mg per day

Mineral	Function	Sources
Calcium	Bone and teeth formation; blood clotting; nerve transmission; important for weight maintenance	Milk, cheese, dark green vegetables, dried legumes
Sodium	Acid-base balance; body water balance; nerve function	Salt
Potassium	Acid-base balance; fluid balance; nerve transmission	Leafy vegetables, cantaloupe, lima beans, potatoes, bananas, milk, meats
Chloride	Acid-base balance; fluid balance; nerve transmission	Salt
Magnesium	Strengthen bones; release of energy	Nuts, eggs, whole grain cereals, leafy green vegetables, seeds, beans, bananas
Phosphorus	Works with calcium to strengthen bones	Dairy products, meat, poultry, eggs, whole grain cereals, legumes
Sulfur	Component of B vitamins thiamin and biotin; helps to stabilize the shape of proteins	Synthesized from protein containing foods

Trace minerals are required in amounts less than 100 mg per day. Common trace minerals include: selenium, iron, copper, zinc, fluorine, iodine, chromium, molybdenum, manganese. Of these trace minerals, iron deficiency is common, especially in females. Iron is important for transporting oxygen to the body, which is especially important for exercise. Iron can be found in eggs, lean meat, legumes, whole grains and dark green leafy vegetables.

Water

Water is vital for our survival. We can go weeks without food, but we can only survive a few days without water. Water has many functions. Water is important in muscle contraction, nerve conduction, waste elimination, joint lubrication, nutrient transport, metabolism and proper fluid balance.

About 50–70% of a healthy individual's body weight is water. As we age, our body water decreases. In addition, males usually have a higher percentage of their total body mass coming from water than females. This difference is due to the amount of lean muscle tissue (lean muscle is 70% water) as compared to fat tissue.

The recommended intake for females and males is 2.7 and 3.7 quarts of water each day, respectively. We get this water from liquid, food and metabolism. It is recommended that we drink a minimum of 8 glasses of water a day. We usually consume around 1,350 ml of water in liquid, 1,000 ml from foods, especially fruits and vegetables which have a high water content, and the rest from metabolized water when food nutrients are broken down for energy. Additional water intake will be required during exercise and in hot/humid weather.

The Food Guide Pyramid

The Food Guide Pyramid was updated in 2005 to MyPyramid designed to provide an easy visual means of determining appropriate food choices and amounts. The three groups on the left contain those items that should be the staple of the diet: carbohydrates—whole grain breads, cereals and pastas, as well as fruits and vegetables. Meats, poultry, fish and dairy require fewer servings. Saturated and trans fats as well as processed and simple sugars are to be used "sparingly." Each group on the pyramid has a designated amount based on calorie intake. It is important to know what a serving size is for each group, as an incorrect serving size can result in greater calorie intake. You can eat the right foods, but if your caloric intake is too high and not being burned as fuel (energy), weight gain will result. For a more individualized Pyramid, visit MyPyramid.gov.

Food Guide Pyramid

A Guide To Daily Food Choices

GRAINS	VEGETABLES	FRUITS	MILK	MEAT & BEANS
Make half your grains whole	Vary your veggies	Focus on fruits	Get your calcium-rich foods	Go lean with protein
Eat at least 3 oz. of whole-grain cereals, breads, crackers, rice, or pasta every day

1 oz. is about 1 slice of bread, about 1 cup of breakfast cereal, or ¹/₂ cup of cooked rice, cereal, or pasta | Eat more dark-green veggies like broccoli, spinach, and other dark leafy greens

Eat more orange vegetables like carrots and sweetpotatoes

Eat more dry beans and peas like pinto beans, kidney beans, and lentils | Eat a variety of fruit

Choose fresh, frozen, canned, or dried fruit

Go easy on fruit juices | Go low-fat or fat-free when you choose milk, yogurt, and other milk products

If you don't or can't consume milk, choose lactose-free products or other calcium sources such as fortified foods and beverages | Choose low-fat or lean meats and poultry

Bake it, broil it, or grill it

Vary your protein routine — choose more fish, beans, peas, nuts, and seeds |

For a 2,000-calorie diet, you need the amounts below from each food group. To find the amounts that are right for you, go to MyPyramid.gov.

Eat 6 oz. every day	Eat 2¹/₂ cups every day	Eat 2 cups every day	Get 3 cups every day; for kids aged 2 to 8, it's 2	Eat 5¹/₂ oz. every day

Find your balance between food and physical activity

- Be sure to stay within your daily calorie needs.
- Be physically active for at least 30 minutes most days of the week.
- About 60 minutes a day of physical activity may be needed to prevent weight gain.
- For sustaining weight loss, at least 60 to 90 minutes a day of physical activity may be required.
- Children and teenagers should be physically active for 60 minutes every day, or most days.

Know the limits on fats, sugars, and salt (sodium)

- Make most of your fat sources from fish, nuts, and vegetable oils.
- Limit solid fats like butter, stick margarine, shortening, and lard, as well as foods that contain these.
- Check the Nutrition Facts label to keep saturated fats, *trans* fats, and sodium low.
- Choose food and beverages low in added sugars. Added sugars contribute calories with few, if any, nutrients.

MyPyramid.gov
STEPS TO A HEALTHIER YOU

U.S. Department of Agriculture
Center for Nutrition Policy and Promotion
April 2005
CNPP-15

USDA is an equal opportunity provider and employer.

For a look at other countries' food guide pyramids view the following publication online http://www.eatright.org/images/journal/0402/commentary.pdf.

Source: U.S. Department of Agriculture/U.S. Department of Health and Human Services. http://www.mypyramid.gov/downloads/MiniPoster.pdf

How many servings do you need each day?

In the following table you can find the 2005 updated recommended number of servings based on your calorie intake.

	Sedentary women and older adults (1600 calories)	Most children, teenage girls, active women and sedentary men (2,200 calories)	Teenage boys, most active men, some very active women (2,800 calories)	Extremely active men (__ calories)
Calorie level	1,200–1,600	1,800–2,200	2,400–2,800	3,000–3,200
Whole Grains	4–6	7–9	10–11	11
Vegetables	2–3	4	5–6	7
Fruit group	1.5–2	2–3	3–4	5
Low Fat/Skim Milk group	*2–3	*2–3	*2–3	*2–3
Lean Meat and Beans	2–5 oz equivalents**	5–6 oz equivalents**	6–7 oz equivalents**	7 oz equivalents**
Additional Fats	30–33 g (60% from healthy fats)	36–44 g (60% from healthy fats)	46–56 g (60% from healthy fats)	66–79 g (60% from healthy fats)
Additional Sugars	5–6 tsp	8–12 tsp	14–18 tsp	20–28 tsp

*Women who are pregnant or breastfeeding, teenagers, and young adults to age 24 need 3 servings.
**The following count as 1 ounce equivalents: 1 ounce meat, poultry, or fish; 1 egg; ½ cup cooked dry beans or tofu; 2 tbsp peanut butter; ⅓ cup of nuts; ¼ cup of seeds.
http://www.cnpp.usda.gov/pyramid-update/FGP%20docs/TABLE%201.pdf

How to determine a serving size

Here are some tips to help you correctly estimate the size of your food portions. You may need to use measuring spoons and cups at first to have an accurate measure.

Food serving	Serving size equivalent
1 teaspoon of margarine/butter	tip of your thumb
1 ounce of cheese	your thumb or four dice stacked together
3 ounces of meat	a deck of cards, the palm of your hand, or an audiocassette tape
½ cup of rice or cooked vegetables	an ice cream scoop
2 tablespoons of peanut butter	a Ping-Pong ball
1 cup of pasta	a woman's fist or a tennis ball
1 medium potato	a computer mouse
1 apple/peach/orange/pear	a baseball.

How to Understand and Use the Nutrition Facts Label

Now that you understand how to read the MyPyramid and how to determine your number of servings from each food group, how can you determine if you are meeting these recommendations? If you are buying food, it is important to know how to read package labels. By knowing how to read the food facts on the food label, you will be able to make wise choices and meet the daily recommendations.

Sample label for Macaroni and Cheese

http://www.cfsan.fda.gov/,dms/foodlab.html

1. The serving size: The first place you should look on the food label is the serving size and the number of servings in the package. In the sample label of macaroni and cheese, if you ate the whole package, you would have eaten two cups and therefore need to multiple the calories and other nutrient amounts by two.

2. Calories (and calories from fat): In this section you will find the number of total calories per serving as well as the number of calories that come from fat. In the sample label of macaroni and cheese, notice that almost half the calories come from fat.

3. Limit these nutrients: This section lists nutrients that Americans get in adequate or more than adequate amounts and that are associated with diseases. Trans fat is a recent addition to this section.

4. Get enough of these: The nutrients listed in this section of the food label are important nutrients for reducing the risk of disease. Most individuals do not get enough of these.

5. Footnote: The footnote defines the percent Daily Values based on a 2,000 calorie diet. It shows the recommended amounts of certain nutrients based on a 2,000 and 2,500 calorie diet.

6. Percent Daily Value (%DV): The %DV are based on the daily value recommendations for key nutrients based on a 2,000 calorie diet. The %DV helps you to determine if a serving of food is high or low in a nutrient. (Trans fat does not have a %DV).

When reading labels, it is also important to read through the ingredients list. Ingredients are listed in descending order of weight. By looking through the ingredients you can determine if sugars, fats, especially trans fats, and other additives and chemicals have been added to the product. It is useful to compare similar products to find a product that has the most natural and best quality ingredients.

Dietary Guidelines for Americans

In 1980, the U.S. Department of Health and Human Services (HHS) and the U.S. Department of Agriculture (USDA) joined efforts to provide science-based advice for reducing risk of diseases and promoting health through a proper diet and physical activity. These recommendations are called the Dietary Guidelines for Americans and are updated every five years. Below you will find the current recommendations, updated in 2005.

Dietary Guidelines For Americans, 2005

(A) Aim for Fitness	Aim for a healthy weight.
	Be physically active each day for minimum of 30 minutes.
	Physical Activity should include all components of fitness: cardiorespiratory endurance, muscular strength and endurance, and flexibility.
(B) Build a Healthy Base	Consume a variety of foods; use the Food Guide Pyramid as a tool for balancing intake of food groups.
	Choose a variety of grains daily, especially whole grains, which are higher in fiber.
	Choose a variety of fruits and vegetables daily.
	Choose low-fat or fat-free milk and milk products.
	Keep food safe to eat.
(C) Choose Sensibly	Choose a diet that is low in saturated fat, and cholesterol and minimal in trans fat, with less than 30% from total fat.
	Choose beverages and foods to moderate your intake of sugars.
	Choose and prepare foods with less salt.
	If you drink alcoholic beverages, do so in moderation.

Dietary Reference Intake for Macronutrients

Expanding on the Dietary Reference Intake (DRI), the Food and Nutrition Board's (FNB's) DRI committee created a group to evaluate current knowledge about macronutrients (carbohydrates, proteins, and fats) in the scientific literature. Their goals were four-fold. First, to evaluate what foods provide the best quality macronutrients. Second, to develop intake levels that would influence good nutrition for life and decrease the risk of disease. Three, to evaluate the safety of consuming large quantities of certain macronutrients. Four, to specifically address macronutrient requirements for certain populations.

The Institute of Medicine (IOM) published the dietary Reference Intake for Macronutrients on September 5, 2002.

This report, designed to replace and expand upon the former Recommended Dietary Allowances of the Food and Nutrition Board, establishes ranges for fat, carbohydrates and protein and stresses the importance of balancing diet with exercise. Highlights of the report include:

- Adults should get 45% to 65% of their calories from carbohydrates, 20% to 35% from fat, and 10 to 35% from protein. Acceptable ranges for children are similar to those for adults, except that infants and younger children need a slightly higher proportion of fat (25%–40%).
- To maintain cardiovascular health, regardless of weight, adults and children should achieve a total of at least one hour of moderately intense physical activity each day.
- Added sugars should comprise no more than 25% of total calories consumed. Added sugars are those incorporated into foods and beverages during production, which usually provide insignificant amounts of vitamins, minerals or other essential nutrients. Major sources include soft drinks, fruit drinks, pastries, candy and other sweets.
- The recommended intake for total fiber for adults 50 years and younger is set at 38 grams for men and 25 grams for women, while for men and women over 50 it is 30 and 21 grams per day, respectively, due to decreased food consumption.
- Using new data, the report reaffirms previously established recommended levels of protein intake, which is 0.8 grams per kilogram of body weight for adults; however recommended levels for pregnancy are increased.
- The report doesn't set maximum levels for saturated fat, cholesterol, or trans fatty acids, as increased risk exists at levels above zero; however, the recommendation is to eat as little as possible while consuming a diet adequate in important other essential nutrients.
- Recommendations are made for linoleic acid (an omega-6 fatty acid) and for alpha-linolenic acid (an omega-3 fatty acid).

Institute of Medicine. Dietary Reference Intakes for Macronutrients Report. September 5, 2002.

Weight Management

With the majority of Americans overweight and obese, achieving and maintaining a healthy body weight is a big concern. The more important issue is controlling the amount of body fat. An individual is categorized as overweight or obese based on body mass index or BMI. BMI is defined as the ratio of your weight in pounds over your height in inches squared. Below you will find the BMI equation, an example, and the BMI ranges.

$$BMI = (Weight\ in\ pounds/(height\ in\ inches)^2) \times 703$$

For example, a person who weighs 200 pounds and is 6 feet tall has a BMI of 27.1.

$$BMI = (200\ lbs./(72\ inches)^2) \times 703 = 27.1$$

BMI	Weight Status
under 18.5	Underweight
18.5–24.9	Normal
25.0–29.9	Overweight
over 30.0	Obese

Two people can have the same BMI, but a different body fat percentage. A body-builder with a large muscle mass and a low percentage body fat may have the same BMI as a person who has more body fat because BMI is calculated using only the factors of weight and height. These men have the same height, weight, and BMI, however, their body fat percentage is very different.

	6'3"	Height	6'3"	
	220 lbs	Weight	220 lbs	
	27.5	BMI	27.5	

Body weight is maintained by consuming the same number of calories you expend each day. An individual's body weight increases when the number of calories consumed over a period of time is consistently greater than the number of calories expended each day. An individual's body weight will decrease when the number of calories consumed over a period of time is consistently less than the number of calories expended each day.

Calorie expenditure can be broken down into three different components, basal metabolic rate (BMR), food digestion, and physical activity. BMR accounts for 55–75% of total energy expenditure (TEE) each day. BMR is the amount of energy required to maintain the function of vital organs at rest. BMR is most affected by muscle mass. Individuals with a higher percentage of muscle mass will have a higher BMR, therefore, males will have a higher BMR than females. As we age our BMR decreases due to decreases in muscle mass. The digestion of food requires energy and makes up 5–15% of TEE. Physical activity is the component that we have the most control over. It accounts for 10–40% of TEE each day. Exercise results in a temporary increase in BMR.

Your BMR can be determined by indirect calorimetry in a laboratory setting, by measuring the amount of carbon dioxide you expend. This requires time and money. The MedGem is a cheaper, less cumbersome and accurate method of determining BMR that analyzes the amount of oxygen you breath. This option is becoming more widely available. A free and simple way to determine your BMR is to estimate it by using the worksheet in Appendix E. An estimate of your activity level can be determined by utilizing the worksheets in Appendix D.

The overall process of losing weight or maintaining weight seems very simple; however, many individuals struggle with maintaining a healthy body weight. Much of this struggle is due to lack of education of what a balanced diet should consist of, how many servings should be consumed from the various food groups and most importantly, how much is a serving size. While their weight was gained over a period of time, most individuals want to have a rapid weight loss. As a result of the desire for a quick fix, a number of diets, pills, and surgical procedures have been developed to satisfy the desire of many Americans to lose weight. Some current popular diets are compared and evaluated in the following table.

Comparison and Evaluation of Current Popular Diets

Diet	Principle	Advantages	Disadvantages	Comments
Atkins: low carb/ high fat	50–75% protein & fat 25–50% complex carb 3 phases: induction, wt. loss, maintenance	Some people may enjoy eating meat and fatty foods.	Food choices are high in fat, from animal sources, which also means high in cholesterol.	Difficult to adhere to and to sustain over a long period of time
South Beach Diet: Low glycemic carbs, low saturated fat	3 phases: carb elimination, slowly reintroduce carbs, maintenance	Emphasizes reducing bad fats and increasing good fats.	Improper usage of the glycemic index in identifying carbohydrates	First phase of diet is not necessary and may be harmful to some
The Zone Diet: low carb, high protein, moderate fat	Eating a specific balance of carbs/ proteins/fats at each meal	Eating multiple meals a day; stresses fruits/ vegetables and low glycemic index foods.	Must calculate meal portions to have exact balance; restrictive in calories	Low in whole grains and calcium rich foods; low calorie intake results in deficiency in important vitamins and minerals
Pritikin: Low Fat/ Low calorie	Unprocessed fruits, vegetables, lean meats, non-fat dairy and low-fat carbs	Encourages fruits and vegetables and eating frequently.	Very lowfat intake may be difficult to maintain	Nutritionally sound if you choose a variety of foods
Weight Watchers: point system	Food point system and group motivation	Weekly meetings, weigh-ins, choose foods based on points	Correctly translating non-Weight Watcher foods to correct points	Promotes healthy eating and manageable weight loss
Beverly Hills Diet: specific foods & combinations	Foods need to be eaten separately, loss 10–15 lbs in 35 days	You eat less because of fewer choices.	Not a sustainable diet	Encourages unsafe eating practices Not a healthy approach
Glucose Revolution:	Based on glycemic index of foods	Encourages heart-healthy fats, limits high fat meats and saturated fats	Understanding what the glycemic index is for foods	Promotes healthy eating

Overall, many popular diets are based on a negative energy balance, meaning you consume fewer calories than you expend. Many individuals do experience rapid weight loss with the diets currently available, however, the majority of this rapid weight lost is due to water weight loss. As a result of the restrictive nature of the diet or high consumption of certain foods, many individuals are unable to sustain the diet and return to their old habits. Since they were not properly educated, when individuals return to their normal diet habits after experimenting with a new diet, the result is gaining back the weight lost and perhaps even more. This is termed weight cycling, especially if the individual attempts many diets.

Individuals who are confused about all the information they are constantly bombarded with through the media, should speak with a licensed dietician and develop a nutrition and exercise plan that is appropriate for them. A number of studies have shown that following a well-balanced diet, as described in this chapter, and expending energy through regular physical activity is the best way to lose and maintain a healthy body weight.

Review Questions

1. Of the six essential nutrients, which ones provide energy and how many calories per gram do they provide?
2. What are the ABCs of the Dietary Guidelines for Americans?
3. What are the fat-soluble vitamins?
4. Which type(s) of fats are considered to be healthy fats, saturated, trans, monounsaturated or polyunsaturated?
5. What type of foods should make up the foundation of the diet, 40–60%? (hint: look at the MyPyramid)
6. To determine how many servings are in a package, where do you look?

How is your diet?

Evaluate how much of your diet comes from convenience-packaged foods/fast foods and how much comes from fresh fruit, vegetables and whole grains. What can you do to improve your diet?

To get an idea of your overall food intake, keep a food record for one week (use the sheets located in Appendix F). Once you have completed this record, you can enter your food record at the following site, http://www.ag.uiuc.edu/~food-lab/nat/mainnat.html, to get a breakdown of your overall food intake, including vitamins, minerals, calorie intake, etc.

References

Books

Agatston, Arthur (2003). *The South Beach Diet.* Emmaus, Pa: Rodale, Inc.

Atkins, Robert C. (2001). *Dr. Atkins' New Diet Revolution.* Avon Books. New York, NY.

Brand-Miller, Jennie; Wolever, Thomas, M.S.; Foster-Powell, Kaye; and Calagiuri, Stephen. (2002). *The New Glucose Revolution.* Marlow & Company. New York, NY.

Campbell, T. Colin (2005). *The China Study,* First Edition. BenBella Books. Dallas, Texas.

Clark, Nancy (1997). *Nancy Clark's Sports Nutrition Guidebook,* 2nd edition. Champaign, IL: Human Kinetics.

Fahey, Thomas D.; Insel, Paul M.; & Roth, Walton T. (2001). *Fit & Well,* 4th edition. Mountain View, CA: Mayfield Publishing Company.

Franz, Marion J. (1994). *Fast Food Facts.* 4th edition. Minneapolis, MN: Chronimed Publishing.

Gershoff, Stanley (1990). *The Tufts University Guide to Total Nutrition.* New York, NY: Harper and Row Publishers.

Maughan, Ronald J. & Burke, Louise M. (2002). *Sports Nutrition.* Malden, MA: Blackwell Science Ltd.

Mayers, Jean (1990). *Diet and Nutrition Guide.* New York, NY: Scripps Howard Company.

Netzer, Corinne, T. (1994). *The Complete Book of Food Counts.* New York, NY: Dell Publishing.

Thompson, Janice & Manore, Melinda (2005). *Nutrition: An Applied Approach.* San Francisco, CA: Benjamin Cummings.

Pritikin, Robert (1999). *The Pritikin Weight Loss Breakthrough.* Signet Books. New York, NY.

Sears, Barry & Lawren, Bill (1995). *The Zone.* New York, NY: HarperCollins Publishers, Inc.

Wardlaw, Gordon M.; Insel, Paul M.; & Seyler, Marcia F. (1994). *Contemporary Nutrition Issues and Insights.* St. Louis, MO: Mosby-Year Book, Inc.

Wildman, Robert & Miller, Barry (2004). *Sports and Fitness Nutrition.* Belmont, CA: Wadsworth/Thompson Learning.

Newsletters

"Harvard Women's Health Watch." Harvard Medical School Health Publications Group, 164 Longwood Avenue, Boston, MA 02115. E-mail HWH@Warren.Med.Harvard.Edu.

"Nutrition Action Health Letter." Center for Science in the Public Interest, Suite 300, 1875 Connecticut Avenue, NW, Washington, DC 20009–5728.

"Tufts University Diet and Nutrition Letter." Tufts Diet and Nutrition Letter. P.O. Box 57857, Boulder, CO 80322–7857. Customer Service: 1–800–274–7581.

"University of California at Berkeley Wellness Letter." Health Letter, P.O. Box 420148, Palm Coast, FL 32142. Telephone: (904) 445–6414.

Government Publications

U.S. Department of Agriculture

Human Nutrition Information Service

Nutrition Education Division

Belcrest Road

Hyattsville, MD 20782

Telephone: (301) 436–5724

Institute of Medicine. *Dietary Reference Intakes for Macronutrients Report.* September 5, 2002.

Web Sites

www.iom.edu/report.asp?id=4340 Institutes of Medicine 2002 Report

www.hsph.harvard.edu/nutritionsource/pyramids.html Comparing Pyramids

www.pueblo.gsa.gov/cic_text/food/food-pyramid/main.htm Food Guide Pyramid

http://www.nhlbi.nih.gov/guidelines/obesity/ob_home.htm Obesity Guidelines

http://www.cfsan.fda.gov/~dms/foodlab.html Reading Food Labels

http://www.recoverymedicine.com/hydrogenated_oils.htm Trans fat

http://www.health.gov/dietaryguidelines/dga2005/document/ 2005 Dietary Guidelines

http://www.ag.uiuc.edu/~food-lab/nat/mainnat.html Online food record evaluation

http://www.cnpp.usda.gov/pyramid-update/FGP%20docs/TABLE%201.pdf Food Guide Pyramid Updates

http://www.nhmrc.gov.au/publications/diet/n6p4.htm / Estimating Energy Requirements (Australia)

http://www.nutritiondata.com Nutrition Facts & Calorie Counter

Cardiovascular Wellness

Inquiries

1. Have any of your relatives suffered from cardiovascular disease? If so, in what way, and what are you doing to prevent the same situation in your life?

_____

_____

_____

Responses of Others

_____

_____

2. What is your current blood pressure reading? What is your current cholesterol level (with ratio of total to HDL)?

_____

Responses of Others

_____

_____

Cardiovascular disease is a disease of the heart and blood vessels. It is considered one of the leading causes of death in the United States. The major form of cardiovascular disease is coronary heart disease (CHD). In coronary heart disease, the arteries supplying the heart with oxygen and nutrients become lined with fatty deposits that build up over a period of time and restrict the capability of the system to work to its fullest potential. Severe blockage may result in a heart attack or stroke. Approximately 1.5 million heart attacks occur each year, and 500,000 result in death.

Risk Factors for CHD

The American Heart Association (AHA) suggests that risk factors for CHD are grouped into two categories: primary or major risk factors and secondary or contributing risk factors. Primary risk factors have been found to have a direct relationship to coronary heart disease while secondary risk factors contribute to CHD, but their exact contribution has yet to be determined.

Primary Risk Factors

Cigarette Smoking

Medical professionals consider cigarette smoking the most harmful of the preventable risk factors associated with chronic illness and premature death. Cigarette smoking is responsible for one of every five deaths annually in the United States. It contributes to approximately 430,000 premature deaths from cardiovascular and pulmonary diseases, not to mention cancer related deaths. Smoking increases heart rate and blood pressure while restricting blood flow, making it easier for fatty deposits to form on arterial walls and increasing the chance that blockage may occur.

High Cholesterol

The risk of coronary heart disease increases as cholesterol levels increase. Cholesterol is a fatty, wax-like substance that circulates through the bloodstream and is necessary for proper functioning of the body. Our bodies obtain cholesterol in two ways: from the liver, which manufactures it, and from the foods we eat. Cholesterol levels vary depending on diet, age, gender, heredity and other factors.

Cholesterol is carried in protein-lipid packages called lipoproteins. Low-density Lipoproteins (LDL) shuttle cholesterol from the liver to the organs that require it. LDL is known as "bad" cholesterol because if there is more than the body can use, the excess is deposited in the blood vessels. When it accumulates, it can block arteries and cause heart attacks and strokes. High-density Lipoproteins (HDL) or "good" cholesterol, shuttle unused cholesterol back to the liver for recycling. Those with a cholesterol level below 200 mg/dl are considered at low risk for developing CHD. High LDL levels and low HDL levels are associated with a high risk for CHD. HDL is especially important because a high HDL level seems to offer protection from CHD even in cases where total cholesterol is high. The ratio of total cholesterol to high-density lipoproteins is considered one of the best indicators predicting cardiovascular disease.

High Blood Pressure

High blood pressure occurs when too much force or pressure is exerted against the wall of the arteries. If your blood pressure is high, your heart has to work harder to push the blood throughout your system. Over time, a strained and over-taxed heart may weaken and enlarge. Increased blood pressure may also scar and harden arteries. Generally, a systolic blood pressure over 140mm Hg or a diastolic pressure over 90mm Hg is considered high. Keys to controlling blood pressure are regular aerobic exercise, weight control, smoking cessation and a low fat and low salt diet.

Physical Inactivity

The American Heart Association has officially recognized physical inactivity as a major risk factor for cardiovascular disease. An estimated 35 to 50 million Americans are sedentary increasing their risk for developing CVD. Exercise is thought to be the closest thing to a "magic bullet" against heart disease. Research suggests that regular vigorous aerobic exercise 3 to 4 times a week not only decreases a person's chance of developing CHD, but also improves a person's chance of survival if they have a heart attack. Aerobic exercise can also help negate other primary and secondary risk factors such as high cholesterol, high blood pressure, obesity, diabetes and stress.

Family History

One risk is a history of first-degree male relatives (father, grandfather or brothers) who have had coronary heart disease or who died of coronary heart disease before the age of 55. Also, first-degree female relatives (mother, grandmother, or sisters) who have had coronary heart disease or who died of coronary heart disease before the age of 65 indicates a strong familial tendency. These people are strongly encouraged to keep the other risk factors as low as possible.

Gender

Men, as compared to women, are more likely to develop coronary heart disease before age 40. Before age 40, it is thought that estrogen protects a woman against CHD. An alarming trend is the increased incidence of heart attacks in pre-menopausal women who have been smoking long enough for it to affect their health, especially when combined with oral contraceptive use.

Obesity

Obese individuals make up over 30% of the American adult population. Individuals are considered obese if they have a body mass index (BMI) over 30, or over 24% body fat in males and over 28% body fat in females. Due to excess body weight and fat, a greater strain is placed on the heart. In general, most obese individuals are not active, therefore they are more susceptible to problems associated with other risk factors such as high blood pressure, high cholesterol and diabetes. For those who are obese, losing even a small amount, such as 10%, of their body weight can have very beneficial effects on cardiovascular health, including a reduction in blood pressure.

Increasing Age

The risk of developing coronary heart disease is greater as one gets older. Half of heart attacks occur in people 65 or older. This is due to the fact that plaque (fatty deposits) has had more years to collect on the arterial walls. In addition, as people age, they may have a tendency to exercise less and under utilize the cardiovascular system.

Secondary Risk Factors

Diabetes

Diabetes is a disease characterized by high blood sugar (glucose) levels. Over 80% of diabetics die from some form of cardiovascular disease. This may be due to the fact that most diabetics have trouble metabolizing fat, which may lead to an increased buildup of fatty deposits on the linings of the arterial walls. A person can help control the risk associated with diabetes by increasing physical activity and monitoring diet. In Type 1 diabetes, no insulin is produced, and so it must be injected daily. Type 1 diabetes occurs early in life. Type 2 diabetes occurs most often in middle-aged, overweight, sedentary adults, as well as overweight, sedentary youth. Excessive weight is a factor because it increases cellular resistance to insulin. In contrast, exercise decreases insulin resistance. Type 2 diabetes makes up approximately 90% of all individuals diagnosed with diabetes. Data indicate that at least 75% of new cases of type 2 diabetes can be prevented through regular exercise and maintaining normal weight. Diabetes has numerous long-range complications, which primarily involve degenerative disorders of the blood vessels and nerves.

Stress

Excessive stress can increase a person's chance of developing CHD. Chronic stress places a constant strain on the cardiovascular system, which can lead to CHD. Stress increases both the cholesterol in the blood as well as blood pressure. Individuals under excessive stress tend to be smokers. Generally, Type A personalities (high-achievers who are hurried, competitive and angry) tend to have a higher incidence of coronary heart disease.

After examining the primary and secondary risk factors, there are certain lifestyle changes that, if adopted, can help prevent future coronary heart disease. These lifestyle changes include the following:

- Do not smoke.
- Adopt or follow a low-fat and low-salt diet.
- Maintain an appropriate body weight.
- Exercise on a regular basis.
- Learn to cope and manage stress.
- Have a yearly physical examination by a well-trained physician.

Managing Serum Cholesterol Levels

Everyone should be aware of their total serum cholesterol. Ask your doctor if dietary modifications and increased physical activity are recommended when making a regular office visit.

Fats

1. Consume less than 10% of calories from saturated fatty acids, less than 300 mg/day of cholesterol, and keep trans fatty acid consumption as low as possible.
2. Keep total fat intake between 20–35% of calories, with most fats coming from sources of polyunsaturated and monounsaturated fatty acids, such as fish, nuts and vegetable oils.
3. Switch to skim milk rather than 2% or whole.
4. Eat less fried food.
5. Avoid foods that include sauces, gravies or oily dressings.
6. Trim all visible fats from meats before and after cooking.
7. Don't eat the skin from poultry; it contains fat and cholesterol.
8. Choose to eat a meatless dish one or two meals per week.
9. Choose low-fat snacks such as fresh fruits, raw vegetables or salt-free pretzels to munch rather than fatty chips, cookies, etc.
10. Eat fish twice a week; baked or broiled, not fried.

Physical Activity

Participate in regular physical activity and reduce sedentary activities to promote health, psychological well-being, and a healthy body weight.

- To reduce the risk of chronic disease in adulthood: participate in at least 30 minutes of moderate-intensity physical activity, above usual activity, at work or home on most days of the week.
- For most people, greater health benefits can be obtained by engaging in physical activity of more vigorous intensity or longer duration.
- To help manage body weight and prevent gradual, unhealthy body weight gain in adulthood: participate in approximately 60 minutes of moderate-to-vigorous activity on most days of the week while not exceeding caloric intake requirements.
- To sustain weight loss in adulthood: engage in at least 60 to 90 minutes of daily moderate-intensity physically activity while not exceeding caloric intake requirements. Some people may need to consult with a healthcare provider before participating in this level of activity.

Achieve physical fitness by including cardiovascular conditioning, stretching exercises for flexibility, and resistance exercises or calisthenics for muscle strength and endurance.

Stop Smoking

If you're ready, Clearing the Air: A Guide to Quitting Smoking, available from the American Cancer Society, offers these recommendations:

1. Identify reasons for quitting.
2. Set a target date for quitting.
3. Identify your barriers to quitting.
4. Make specific plans ahead of time for dealing with temptations.
5. Change to a brand you find distasteful.
6. Involve friends and family.
7. On the day you quit, toss out all cigarettes and matches.
8. After you quit, change your normal routine and location associated with smoking.
9. When you get the "crazies," chew gum, carrots, sunflower seeds, etc.
10. Mark progress; celebrate anniversaries.

Risk Profile–Lipid and Lipoprotein Concentrations

Total Cholesterol	Risk
<200 mg/dl	Desirable
200 to 239 mg/dl	Borderline
>240 mg/dl	High

LDL Cholesterol	Risk
<100 md/dl	Optimal
100 to 129 mg/dl	Near optimal/above optimal
130 to 159 mg/dl	Borderline high
160 to 189 mg/dl	High
>190 mg/dl	Very High

HDL Cholesterol	Risk
40 mg/dl	Increased risk
60 mg/dl	Heart protective

Triglycides	Risk
150 mg/dl	Normal
150 to 199 mg/dl	Borderline high
200 to 499 mg/dl	High
>500 mg/dl	Very High
< is less than	
≥ is equal to or greater than	
≤ is equal to or less than	

Adapted from "Revised Cholesterol Guidelines, July, 2001, Harvard Heart Letter.

Classification of Blood Pressure for Adults Age 18 Years and Older

Category	Systolic (mmHg)	Diastolic (mmHg)
Optimal		
	120 to 129	80 to 84
High normal	**130 to 139**	85 to 89
Hypertension		
Stage 1 (mild)	140 to 159	90 to 99
Stage 2 (moderate)	160 to 179	100 to 109
Stage 3 (severe)	180 to 209	110 to 119
Stage 4 (very severe)	>210	>120

Review Questions

1. What are the primary risk factors for CHD?
2. Which of these factors can you control?
3. What are acceptable levels for triglycides, LDL, HDL and total cholesterol?
4. What is your Body Mass Index?
5. How can the information in this chapter help you make better health decisions?

References

ACSM's *Guidelines for Exercise Testing and Prescription.* (2004). Seventh Edition, Philadelphia, PA.

American Heart Association (1998). *Risk Factors and Coronary Heart Disease. AHA Scientific Position.* Dallas, TX: American Heart Association.

Aspaugh, David; Hamrick, M.; & Rosato, F. (2003). *Wellness: Concepts and Applications.* First Edition. New York, NY: McGraw-Hill Higher Education.

Donatelle, R.; Snow-Harter, C.; & Wilcox, A. (1995). *Wellness: Choices for Health and Fitness.* Redwood City, CA: Benjamin/Cummings Publishing Co.

Fahey, Thomas; Insel, P.; & Roth, W. (2001). *Fit and Well.* Mountain View, CA: Mayfield Publishing Company.

Greenberg, J.; Dintiaman, G.; & Myers-Oakes, B. (1995). *Physical Fitness and Wellness.* Needham Heights, MA: Allyn and Bacon.

Hockey, Robert V. (1996). *Physical Fitness: The Pathways to Healthful Living.* St. Louis, MO: Mosby-Year Book, Inc.

Hoeger, Werner and Hoeger, Sharon (1999). *Fitness and Wellness.* Englewood, CO: Morton Publishing Co.

Powers, S. Dodd (2003). *Total Fitness and Wellness,* Brief Edition. Pearson Education, Inc, published as Benjamin Cummings, San Francisco.

Powers, Scott Howley (2001). *Exercise Physiology: Theory and Application to Fitness and Performance.* Fourth Edition, New York, NY: McGraw Hill.

Powers, S. and Dodd, S. (1996). *Total Fitness: Exercise, Nutrition, and Wellness.* Needham Heights, MA: Allyn and Bacon.

Prentice, William (1999). *Fitness and Wellness for Life.* Boston, MA: WCB/McGraw-Hill.

Robbins, G.; Powers, D.; & Burgess, S. (2002). *A Wellness Way of Life.* Fifth Edition, New York, NY: McGraw-Hill Higher Education.

Seiger, L.; Vanderpool, K.; & Barnes, D. (1995). *Fitness and Wellness Strategies.* Dubuque, IA: William C. Brown Communications, Inc.

Stress Management

Inquires

1. What are some sources of stress and distress in your daily life? Explain the physical and emotional responses you have to each stressor.

_____

_____

_____

_____

Responses of Others

_____

_____

2. How might you reduce the negative impact of the stressors you listed above?

_____

Responses of Others

_____

_____

What Is Stress?

The term stress comes from the Latin word stringere, meaning "to draw tight." Stress is the responses that occur in the body when a stressor or stimulus is present. Stress occurs when the body's internal balance is broken or disrupted.

Stress is inevitable. Stress is needed to perform daily tasks of life, and more importantly, to stimulate growth and development. Stress can be beneficial. However, too much stress, especially when it exists for a prolonged period of time and is unrelieved, can result in physical and mental illness.

Dr. Hans Selye, biologist and endocrinologist, defined stress as the "nonspecific response of the body to any demand made upon it." He further points out that stress is caused or triggered by stressors that may be physical, social or psychological and that may be negative or positive in nature.

Selye called human reactions to positive stressors eustress, that is, stress that is beneficial, and he used the term distress to describe detrimental responses to negative stressors. Often there is a fine line between whether something produces eustress or distress. For example, moderate physical training is a stressor that can make you become stronger and more fit. However, if you do too much too soon, it can produce distress in the form of soreness or injury.

Sometimes the difference between eustress and distress is only a matter of interpretation; do you interpret the stressor as a threat or a challenge? Although we may habitually respond in ways that seem automatic and beyond our control, we can choose to examine the way we think and then work on changing counterproductive thinking or beliefs.

Stress should not, however, be considered solely as a physiological phenomenon. Stress has also been viewed from a psychological or cognitive perspective. Current research suggests that the stress response is not a simple biological response to nonspecific stressors but is instead an inter-related process that includes the presence of a stressor, the circumstances in which the stressor occurs, the interpretation of the situation by the person, his or her typical reaction, and the resources available to deal with the stressor. For example, one person may find downhill skiing fun and exciting, and look forward to taking winter vacations to ski the slopes. Another person may have tried to ski, but because of dislike of cold weather and fear of injury, finds skiing a distressing activity. Therefore the stress response in a given situation is dependent upon the individual's perceptions.

I. Psychological or Cognitive Response to Stress

Once the stress process is stimulated by the presence of a stressor, psychological or cognitive processes take over, determining the manner in which the stressor is perceived. An individual's perceptions of a particular situation can elicit a response that may vary from arousal to anxiety. Arousal is the body's heightened awareness that a stressor is present and is a signal to higher centers in the brain to respond (physiological). Anxiety, on the other hand, is described by Speilberger as feelings of tension, apprehension, nervousness and worry. He maintains that these are cognitive rather than biological responses.

The degree to which a particular situation elicits an emotional response depends to a great extent on how the individual appraises the situation and how well prepared he or she feels to handle it. Those individuals who are prone to stress tend to make extreme, absolute, global judgments and engage in cognitive distortions in which they overemphasize the most negative aspects of a given situation. Our thought processes seem automatic, but we need to emphasize the necessity of examining our beliefs and working on changing them when they are erroneous or counterproductive.

Certainly there are both biological and cognitive responses to stressors. Even though we talk about them as two separate processes, they are inter-related and occur simultaneously.

II. Physiological Response to Stress

The General Adaptation Syndrome (GAS)

GAS? It is a sequenced physiological response to the presence of a stressor; the alarm, resistance, recovery, and exhaustion stages of a stress response.

The Alarm Stage (also known as the fight-or-flight response).

Once exposed to any event that is seen as threatening, the body immediately prepares for difficulty. Involuntary changes are controlled by hormonal and nervous system functions and quickly prepare the body for the fight-or-flight response. During this stage, the sympathetic nervous system, which is regulated by the hypothalamus, causes the body to do the following:

- Increase heart rate
- Increase force with which heart contracts
- Dilate coronary arteries
- Constrict abdominal arteries
- Dilate pupils
- Dilate bronchial tubes
- Increase strength of skeletal muscles
- Release glucose from liver
- Increase mental activity
- Significantly increase basal metabolic rate

The Resistance Stage

The second stage of response to a stressor, the resistance stage, reflects the body's attempt to reestablish internal balance, or a state of homeostasis. The high level of energy seen in the initial alarm stage cannot be maintained very long. The body therefore attempts to reduce the intensity of the initial response to a more manageable level. This is accomplished by reducing the production of adrenocorticotropic hormone (ACTH), thus allowing specificity of adaptation to occur. Specific organ systems become the focus of the body's response, such as the cardiovascular and digestive systems.

The Recovery Stage

Because of the ability to move from an alarm stage into a less damaging resistance stage, effective coping or a change in the status of the stressor will probably occur. In fact, as control over the stressful situation is gained, homeostasis is even more completely established and movement toward full recovery is seen. At the completion of the recovery stage, the body has returned to its pre-stressed state and there is minimal evidence of the stressor's existence.

The Exhaustion Stage

Body adjustments required as a result of long-term exposure to a stressor often result in an overload. Specific organs and body systems that were called on during the resistance stage may not be able to resist a stressor indefinitely. This results in exhaustion, and the stress-producing hormone levels rise again. In extreme or chronic cases, exhaustion can become so pronounced that death can occur.

The following table will help you identify some of the physiological changes that take place in your body during stress. Indicate how often each of the physical symptoms happen to you.

Physiological Reactions to Stress

Circle the number that best represents the frequency of occurrence of the following physical symptoms and add up the total number of points.

	Never	Infrequently (More than Once in Six Months)	Occasionally (More than Once per Month)	Very Often (More than Once per Week)	Constantly
1. Tension headaches	1	2	3	4	5
2. Migraine (vascular) headaches	1	2	3	4	5
3. Stomachaches	1	2	3	4	5
4. Increase in blood pressure	1	2	3	4	5
5. Cold hands	1	2	3	4	5
6. Acidic stomach	1	2	3	4	5
7. Shallow, rapid breathing	1	2	3	4	5
8. Diarrhea	1	2	3	4	5
9. Palpitations	1	2	3	4	5
10. Shaky hands	1	2	3	4	5
11. Burping	1	2	3	4	5
12. Gassiness	1	2	3	4	5
13. Increased urge to urinate	1	2	3	4	5
14. Sweaty feet/hands	1	2	3	4	5
15. Oily skin	1	2	3	4	5
16. Fatigue/exhausted feeling	1	2	3	4	5
17. Panting	1	2	3	4	5
18. Dry mouth	1	2	3	4	5
19. Hand tremor	1	2	3	4	5
20. Backache	1	2	3	4	5
21. Neck stiffness	1	2	3	4	5
22. Gum chewing	1	2	3	4	5
23. Grinding teeth	1	2	3	4	5
24. Constipation	1	2	3	4	5
25. Tightness in chest or heart	1	2	3	4	5
26. Dizziness	1	2	3	4	5
27. Nausea/vomiting	1	2	3	4	5
28. Menstrual distress	1	2	3	4	5
29. Skin blemishes	1	2	3	4	5
30. Heart pounding	1	2	3	4	5
31. Colitis	1	2	3	4	5
32. Asthma	1	2	3	4	5
33. Indigestion	1	2	3	4	5
34. High blood pressure	1	2	3	4	5
35. Hyperventilation	1	2	3	4	5
36. Arthritis	1	2	3	4	5
37. Skin rash	1	2	3	4	5
38. Bruxism/jaw pain	1	2	3	4	5
39. Allergy	1	2	3	4	5

Source: H. Ebel et al., eds., Presidential Sports Award Fitness Manual, 197, 208, 98. Copyright 1983 FitCom Corporation, Havertown, PA.

Interpretation

40–75	Low physiological symptoms of stress response
76–100	Moderate physiological symptoms of stress response
101–150	High physiological symptoms of stress response
Over 150	Excessive physiological symptoms of stress response

Personality and Stress

In identifying people who are at risk for developing cardiovascular disease, researchers believed that there was a connection between behavior pattern and risk of heart disease. People were classified as being either "Type A" or "Type B" personalities. The Type A person is always "on the go," never satisfied with his or her level of achievement, and appears tense, suffers from a sense of time urgency, and is competitive and impatient. In contrast, the Type B person is more easy-going and relaxed, more patient and satisfied with his or her level of achievement. A newer category, the Type C person, thrives and stays well during stress. The type A person was believed to have a higher risk of developing cardiovascular disease. Recent research suggests that only those Type A individuals who have hostile or angry behavior patterns are at risk. Therefore identifying the sources of anger and hostility in these people and helping them with behavior modification may allow them to cope more effectively with stress.

Type A Behavior Pattern

According to the research of Friedman and Rosenman, Type A individuals are more prone to coronary heart disease. The Type A personality possesses the following characteristics: competitive, verbally aggressive, hard-driving, unable to relax, very time conscious, easily angered and hostile.

Read each of the statements on the scale below and check which behavior best applies to you.

Assess Yourself 2–1

This scale, based on the one developed by Friedman and Rosenman, will give you an estimate of your Type A tendencies.

Directions: Answer the following questions by indicating the response that most often applies to you.

Yes	No	Statement
—	—	1. I always feel rushed.
—	—	2. I find it hard to relax.
—	—	3. I attempt to do more and more in less and less time.
—	—	4. I often find myself doing more than one thing at a time.
—	—	5. When someone takes too long to make their point, I finish their sentence for them.
—	—	6. Waiting in line for anything drives me crazy.
—	—	7. I am always on time or early.
—	—	8. In a conversation, I often clench my fist and pound home important points.
—	—	9. I often use explosive outbursts to accentuate key points.
—	—	10. I am competitive at everything.
—	—	11. I tend to evaluate my success by translating things into numbers.
—	—	12. Friends tell me I have more energy than most people.
—	—	13. I always move, walk and eat quickly.
—	—	14. I bring work home often.
—	—	15. I tend to get bored on vacation.
—	—	16. I feel guilty when I am not being "productive."
—	—	17. I tend to refocus other people's conversations around things that interest me.
—	—	18. I hurry others along in their conversations.
—	—	19. It is agonizing to be stuck behind someone driving too slowly.
—	—	20. I find it intolerable to let others do something I can do faster.

Scoring: Add up the number of items for which you checked yes. The greater the number of yes items, the more likely it is that you are a Type A personality.

Type B Behavior

Type B behavior is the absence of Type A. While the person who exhibits Type B behavior may be ambitious and successful, he or she is generally calmer, more patient and less hurried. Of course, there are gradations within each behavior type. Most of us go back and forth between Type A and Type B as our activities and pressures vary from one day or week to the next. Type A personalities experience a higher continuous stress level than do Type Bs because they are more likely to be stress-seekers and thereby expose themselves to more challenges than do Type Bs. The response to these challenges turns on the sympathetic nervous system and increases secretions of hormones such as norepinephrine, which combine to produce elevated heart rates.

Type C Behavior and Hardiness

Research has also turned attention to those people who tend to thrive and stay well during challenge and difficulty. They are able to interpret challenge and difficulty as positive challenges or opportunities rather than as threats. They tend to be committed rather than detached or alienated. They feel in control of events and their reactions to those events withstand everyday stressors. Salvador Maddi and Suzanne Kobasa of the University of Chicago have identified "a distress resistance pattern." They call it hardiness, consisting of three Cs, relating to attitude or perception: challenge, commitment and control. Type C people tend to engage in regular exercise and are involved in a number of social support groups. Robert Kriegel and Marilyn Kriegel have also identified a Type C behavior, or what they call a C zone, similar to hardiness, which consists of two of Kobasa and Maddi's three Cs, challenge and control, but replaces commitment with confidence.

The type C person has the following pattern:

- **Challenge.** The person interprets a difficult task or change as a challenge rather than as a threat.
- **Confidence.** The person believes in his or her ability to master a difficult problem or challenge, rather than approaching it with self-doubt.
- **Commitment.** The person positively engages with his or her job, family, and friends, rather than feeling alienated.
- **Control.** The person believes in his or her ability to control events and reactions to events, rather than feeling helpless.

Stress Management

In this section, we discuss ten useful ways to turn off stress and also a variety of relaxation techniques that are helpful in stress management. The recommendations that follow are not a universal remedy for stress but may give you some insight into dealing with stress and knowing your limits. You must know when your various frustrations, conflicts, and stresses are getting to you and take appropriate action to limit or modify them.

Turning Off Stress

Here are eleven ways to turn off stress:

1. Try to change how you perceive specific stress-inducing events. For example, the next time you're driving and a person in another car does something foolish, try not to perceive him or her as an enemy who is out to run you off the road but as a friend who has simply made a driving mistake.
2. Try to understand and deal with your anger. Acknowledge your anger to yourself. Learn to differentiate between levels of anger. Try to diagnose the threat that is causing you to be angry—it may be the result of a difference in values or in style and be no real threat to you at all. Finally, try letting go of anger through forgiveness and by canceling the charges against the other person.
3. Take time to relax or mediate. Try to manage your time more effectively so that you don't court stress through disorganized scheduling.
4. Expand your social support system. Contact and try to establish relationships with new people or groups that may be able to give you emotional support.

5. Exercise regularly. Considerable evidence indicates that people who exercise regularly have lower arousal to stress than do people who are less fit. Exercise aids in balancing and stabilizing the physiological consequences of emotional stress. Exercise also maintains your body systems in a fit state so that they are able to effectively handle any additional stress. Exercise also ensures normal fatigue and relaxation.
6. Eat well. Eat regular, well-balanced meals and avoid alcohol and cigarettes.
7. Slow down. Learn to slow your pace of talking, walking, and eating.
8. Don't take on too many responsibilities. Measure success by quality rather than quantity.
9. Don't set unrealistic deadlines. Give yourself enough time to finish tasks and learn to live with unfinished tasks.
10. Practice effective listening. Avoid interrupting out of impatience.
11. Laugh regularly. There is evidence to prove that laughter can reduce or eliminate stress. Hormones are secreted when one laughs. Laughter is like internal jogging. Laughter is like a medicine to the body.

Relaxation Techniques

There probably are times during the day when you just want to unwind, relax, take time out, and turn off anxiety-producing stimuli. Tension manifests itself in muscle contractions, shallow breathing, a clenched jaw, and a variety of other involuntary responses. With a little practice and patience, you can begin to free yourself of tension with such simple relaxation and meditation techniques as the seven-step relaxation program, hatha-yoga, biofeedback, the progressive relaxation exercise, autogenic training, diaphragmatic breathing, massage and acupressure, repetitive prayer, music with relaxation and Tai Chi. It is important to relieve the tensions in both your body and your brain so that they relax as one.

Keep in mind, however, that even though relaxation can reduce arousal to stress and be just as effective as exercise in reducing the stress response, it does not bring with it the physiological advantages of vigorous exercise.

The Seven-Step Relaxation Program

1. Establish a quiet environment. Arrange for things to be as quiet as possible. Avoid having to answer the phone or door or respond to other distracting stimuli.
2. Find a comfortable position. Sit in a comfortable chair or lie on the floor so that you have full body support.
3. Close your eyes. Now use your imagination. Place yourself in a relaxing environment, such as a beach.
4. Maintain a passive attitude. Focus your attention on your sensations. Diffuse your concentration by letting thoughts pass out of your awareness.
5. Take a deep breath. Tighten your muscles for a few seconds.
6. Exhale and relax. Feel the release in tension and the heaviness of your muscles as you exhale and fall into the comfortable position.
7. Repeat steps 1 through 6 two or three times or until you are relaxed. Take fifteen to twenty minutes to achieve complete relaxation, allowing about thirty seconds between each phase.

Diaphragmatic Breathing

Diaphragmatic breathing is a technique that combines relaxation and quieting. This technique is often utilized in Lamaze classes, yoga and TaiChi. Once mastered, diaphragmatic breathing can temporarily lower breathing from a typical rate of 14 to 18 breaths per minute to nearly 4breaths per minute. Diaphragmatic breathing is a three-segment approach. Assume a comfortable position. Lie on the floor with arms by your sides, eyes closed and back straight. Begin breathing from the diaphragm, rather than by lifting the chest. Concentrate. Follow the air pathway as it enters the body and flows deeply into the lower levels of the lungs, and feel the stomach rise as the air leaves the lungs. Concentrate. Follow each ventilation by doing

Sun Salutation

the following; (1) take air into your lungs through the nose and mouth, (2) pause slightly before exhaling, (3) release the air to flow out via the path from which it entered, and (4) pause slightly after exhalation before repeating step 1. Visualize. Relaxation in diaphragmatic breathing is achieved effectively by combining visualization. Although visualization is a matter of individual preference, most people feel that envisioning the air (or clouds) entering the body with each breath, traveling down the path taken by the air, and leaving through the nostrils is very helpful.

College Students and Stress

A majority of college students deal with stress on a daily basis. Pressure to perform well in school can come from parents, teachers, friends and even oneself. Most students take on jobs to either support their lifestyle or pay for tuition. Trying to juggle school and work and find time to create meaningful and lasting relationships can place considerable stress on a college student. In addition, during the college years a young college student is faced with numerous and significant tasks such as:

a. Achieving emotional independence from family
b. Choosing and preparing for a career
c. Preparing for emotional commitment and family life
d. Developing an ethical system

Inability to juggle all these tasks can leave a college student feeling overwhelmed and almost in a state of despair. Too much stress depresses the immonological system. The common health problems often seen in college health facilities, such as the flu and mono, are most likely stress-related. Second to accidents, suicide is the second leading cause of death of college students.

Student Stress Scale

Use the scale below to assess the stress in your life.

The Student Stress Scale represents an adaptation of Holmes and Rahe's Life Event Scale. It has been modified to apply to college-age adults and should be considered a rough indication of stress levels and health consequences.

In the Student Stress Scale, each event, such as beginning or ending school, is given a score that represents the amount of readjustment a person has to make in life as a result of the change. In some studies, people with serious illness have been found to have high scores on similar scales.

To determine your stress score, add the number of points corresponding to the events you have experienced in the past twelve months. Your score indicates your life-change units (LCU). Those with150–199 LCU have a 37% chance of developing stress-related illnesses within a year. Individuals scoring 200–299 LCU have a 79% chance of developing illness or disease.

1. Death of a close family member	_____	100
2. Death of a close friend	_____	73
3. Divorce between parents	_____	65
4. Jail term	_____	63
5. Major personal injury or illness	_____	63
6. Marriage	_____	58
7. Firing from a job	_____	50
8. Failure of an important course	_____	47
9. Change in health of a family member	_____	45
10. Pregnancy	_____	45
11. Sex problems	_____	44
12. Serious argument with close friend	_____	40
13. Change in financial status	_____	39

14. Change of major	_____	39
15. Trouble with parents	_____	39
16. New girlfriend or boyfriend	_____	37
17. Increase in workload at school	_____	37
18. Outstanding personal achievement	_____	36
19. First quarter/semester in college	_____	36
20. Change in living conditions	_____	31
21. Serious argument with an instructor	_____	30
22. Lower grades than expected	_____	29
23. Change in sleeping habits	_____	29
24. Change in social activities	_____	29
25. Change in eating habits	_____	28
26. Chronic car trouble	_____	26
27. Change in the number of family get-togethers	_____	26
28. Too many missed classes	_____	25
29. Change of college	_____	24
30. Dropping of more than one class	_____	23
31. Minor traffic violations	_____	20

Total _____

Warning Signs of Stress

Selye lists stress symptoms that may represent danger signs. Do you ever experience one or more of these symptoms?

Irritability and depression	Stuttering or other speech problems
Heart palpitations	Insomnia
Dryness of throat and mouth	Breathlessness
Impulsive behavior	Sweating
Inability to concentrate	Frequent urination
Feelings of weakness and dizziness	Diarrhea and indigestion
Crying	Migraine headaches
Anxiety	Premenstrual tension or missed menstrual cycles
Emotional tension	Pain in back
Nervous tics	Increased smoking
Vomiting	Loss of appetite
Easily startled by small sounds	Nightmares
Nervous laughter	Fatigue
Trembling hands	

General Guidelines for Stress Reduction

Selye set forth several suggestions for stress reduction, including:

- Try not to be a perfectionist; instead, perform and work within your capabilities.
- Spend your time in ways other than trying to befriend those persons who don't want to experience your love and friendship.
- Enjoy the simple things in life.
- Strive and fight only for those things that are really worthwhile.
- Accent the positive and the pleasant side of life.
- On experiencing a defeat or setback, maintain your self-confidence by remembering past accomplishments and successes.
- Do not delay tackling the unpleasant tasks that must be done; instead, get at them immediately.
- Evaluate people's progress on the basis of their performance.

- Recognize that leaders, to be leaders, must have the respect of their followers.
- Adopt a motto that you will live in a way that will earn your neighbor's love
- Try to live so that your existence will be useful to society.
- Clarify your values.
- Take constructive action to eliminate a source of stress.

Other suggestions:

- Maintain good physical and mental health.
- Accept what you cannot change.
- Serve other people and some worthy cause.
- Share worries with someone you can trust.
- Pay attention to your body.
- Balance work and recreation.
- Improve your qualifications for the realistic goals you aspire to.
- Avoid reliance on drugs and alcohol.
- Don't be narcissistic.
- Manage your time effectively.
- Laugh at yourself.
- Get enough rest and sleep.
- Don't be too hard on yourself.
- Improve your self-esteem.

References

Blonna, Richard (2000). *Coping with Stress in a Changing World.* Second Edition. New York, NY: McGraw Hill Publishing.

Greenberg, J. S. (2002). *Comprehensive Stress Management.* Seventh Edition. New York, NY: McGraw-Hill Publishing.

Greenberg, J.S. (2002). *Your Personal Stress Profile and Activity Workbook.*

Hahn, D.B. & Payne, W.A. (2005). *Focus on Health.* Seventh Edition. New York, NY: McGraw Hill Publishing.

Web Sites

www.stress.org American Institute of Stress
www.apa.org American Psychological Association

Fitness/Sports Related Injuries

Inquiries

1. Have you suffered any injuries that prevented you from engaging in your normal daily activities? If so, discuss the injury and any rehabilitation that was needed for your recovery.

   _____

   _____

   Responses of Others

   _____

   _____

2. When should you consult a physician for an injury you acquire and when should you resort to your own home treatment?

   _____

   _____

   Responses of Others

   _____

   _____

Sports participation has an inherent risk of injury. On the other hand, the health benefits of sports are significant and generally outweigh the risk. Additionally, preventive measures and early injury recognition can minimize injury problems. Most injuries affect the musculoskeletal system, which includes the bones, joints, muscles, tendons and ligaments. Only a few injuries affect miscellaneous structures such as the skin or internal organs. Sports related injuries can be categorized into acute, chronic musculoskeletal injuries and medical problems.

Acute injuries are the result of a single event that causes damage to a part of the musculoskeletal system. Collisions, falls, and awkward movements of joints are the usual causes. Tissues get injured when a joint is forced beyond its normal range of motion or is impacted causing tissue to abnormally compress, causing tissue damage or contusions. Sprains, strains and fractures are common types of acute injuries each affecting different types of musculoskeletal tissues. Please see chart 'Comparison of Different Types of Acute Injuries' for more information. Chronic injuries are not the result of any single event. Chronic injuries are caused by repetitive forces that injure a structure over time. Musculoskeletal structures gradually adapt to repetitive forces by becoming stronger and better able to absorb stress placed on it. However, this adaptation process is slow. If repetitive forces are increased in intensity and/or duration to rapidly, the adaptation process is overwhelmed, the musculoskeletal tissue begins to breakdown and injury ensues. The breakdown can be followed by an inflammatory response which can cause significant, often long lasting pain and disability. Tendonitis,bursitis and stress fractures are common types of chronic injuries each affecting different types of musculoskeletal tissues. Please see chart 'Comparison of Different Types of Chronic Injuries' for more information.

Though many acute and chronic injuries can't be avoided as they are an inherent part of participation in sports, some may be avoided or reduced in severity. Proper warm up and stretching prior to activity can be a key element in avoiding injury. Appropriate, functional and balanced strength and conditioning programs are also important in preparing the body and its tissues for the demands of athletic endeavors.

Sports injuries are not limited to musculoskeletal tissue injury. Often serious medical and systemic conditions, such as, heat illnesses and head injuries can occur. These conditions can be life-threatening if not recognized and treated properly. Non-emergency conditions, such as, blisters and shin splints are also common. Please see chart 'Other Conditions Related to Fitness/Sports Participation' for more information.

Comparison of Different Types of Acute Injuries

Injury Type	Tissue Involved	Degree	Signs	Treatment
Sprain	Ligament/Joints	**1st Degree** • Minimal Pain/Swelling • No structural damage • No joint instability • Normal weight bearing **2nd Degree** • Moderate Pain/Swelling • Some structural damage • Some joint instability • Difficulty bearing weight **3rd Degree** • Severe Pain/Swelling • Complete ligament rupture • Pop/Snap felt • Joint instability • Difficulty bearing weight	•Immediate onset of pain • Often rapid onset of swelling • Tender upon palpation • Discoloration • Decreased range of motion at the involved joint • Difficulty bearing weight or performing everyday activity with involved joint • Feelings of instability	• Rest, ice, compression, elevation (RICE) • Protective bracing to protect involved joint • Possible surgery • Range of motion exercises • Strengthening of muscles surrounding involved joint to improve active stabilization
Strain	Muscle/Tendon	**1st Degree** • Muscle is tender/painful when used • No structural damage **2nd Degree** • Moderate Pain/Swelling • Some structural damage • Difficult to use involved muscle • Discoloration **3rd Degree** • Severe Pain/Swelling • Complete muscle rupture • Use of involved muscle is impossible	• Immediate onset of pain and difficulty using involved muscle • May feel a snap/pop • Muscle spasm • Discoloration • Tender upon palpation • Partial or complete loss of function	• Rest, ice, compression, elevation (RICE) • Anti-inflammatory medications • Analgesics • Range of motion exercises and stretching as pain subsides • Strengthening of involved muscle once full range of motion is restored
Fracture	Bone	**Simple & Non-Displaced** • Simple crack in the bone • No displacement **Simple & Displaced** • Simple crack in the bone • Displacement of bones from their normal position **Comminuted** • Several cracks in the bone • Multiple bone fragments • Usually displaced **Compound or Open** • Bone fragment pierces the skin • Severe pain/tenderness • Deformity of displaced fractures • Bleeding of compound fractures	• May feel pop/snap • Severe pain/tenderness • Deformity in displaced fracture • Bleeding in compound fracture	• Immediate immobilization • Transportation to a facility capable of taking x-rays of the injured area • Cast or brace for non-displaced fractures • Reduction of displaced fracture • Surgery of all compound fractures to avoid infection and to reduce displaced fragments

Comparison of Different Types of Chronic Injuries

Injury Type	Tissue Involved	Signs & Symptoms	Treatment	Common Examples
Tendonitis	Tendon	• Pain with use in and around the tendon • Tenderness with palpation of the tendon • Occasional swelling or thickening of the tendon	• Rest: Decrease the intensity/ duration of the exercise until pain subsides. Complete rest may not be ideal as it takes away the stimulus of the tendon to adapt and heal. Often finding alternative exercises that still use the injured structure is ideal. • Anti-inflammatory medication • Ice • Stretching • Occasionally, a physician may use corticosteroid injections. Must be used with caution as these tend to weaken tendon and increase the likelihood of complete tendon rupture, especially in weight bearing tendons (Achilles tendon among others).	• Achilles tendontitis • Rotator Cuff tendonitis • Tennis Elbow • Little Leaguers Elbow • Patella tendonitis
Stress Fracture	Bone	• Gradually increasing pain over a bone, eventually leading to severe pain that forces athlete to stop exercising • Palpable tenderness on the bone at the site of the stress fracture • Most common in distance runners	• Rest: Avoidance of the aggravating impact activity. Cross training with a non-weight bearing exercise is good to maintain fitness level • Total non-weight bearing or immobilization is rarely needed • Sometimes surgery is needed to stabilize poor healing stress fractures	• Forefoot stress fracture • Tibia or Shin Bone stress fracture • Hip stress fractures
Bursitis	Bursa	• Swelling or thickening of bursa • Palpable tenderness around the bursa	• Rest: Avoidance of the aggravating activity. Cross training is good to maintain fitness level • Stretch the involved tendon causing the friction over the bursa • Anti-inflammatory medication • Protective padding to shield bursa from further irritation	• Achilles bursitis • Shoulder bursitis

Other Conditions Related to Fitness/Sports Participation

Condition	Prevention	Signs & Symptoms	Treatment
Heat Illness	• Gradual Acclimatization • Wear proper, light clothing • Proper hydration • Maintain proper body weight • Be aware of temperature/ humidity and adjust work-outs accordingly	**Heat Cramps** • Sudden painful contraction of muscle tissue • Dehydration • Mineral Imbalance **Heat Exhaustion** • Feeling of weakness • Fatigue • Occasional collapse without loss of consciousness • Profuse sweating **Heat Stroke** • Serious emergency • Collapse • Confusion • Loss of consciousness possible • Elevated core temperature • Decreased or no sweating • Complete shutdown of body's defensive mechanism against overheating	**Heat Cramps** • Stretching of involved muscle tissue • Fluid & electrolyte replenishment • Rest **Heat Exhaustion** • Fluid & electrolyte replenishment • Cooling the body off • Rest **Heat Stroke** • Immediate cooling through removal of clothes, shade, ice or fanning • Call 911 for immediate professional emergency care
Head Injury	• Head injuries cant be completely avoided but may be decreased in severity • Use of helmets in contact sports • Instruction of proper technique of tackling and protecting oneself • A second head injury before a previous injury has healed is more likely to cause permanent damage and be life-threatening	**Mild Injury** • Slight daze affecting athlete momentarily • No loss of consciousness • No loss of memory **Moderate Injury** • Prolonged confusion and/or irritability • No loss of consciousness • Some loss of memory **Severe Injury** • Loss of consciousness • Prolonged confusion and/or irritability • Loss of memory	**Mild Injury** • Can usually return to activity following evaluation by a qualified health care professional **Moderate Injury** • Should not return to activity until symptoms reside and is evaluated and cleared by a qualified health care professional **Severe Injury** • Immobilization due to possible spinal injury • Call 911 for immediate professional emergency care • Can be life-threatening • Should not return to activity until symptoms reside and is evaluated and cleared by a qualified health care professional
Blisters	• Socks with no prominent seams • Properly fitting shoes • Use of a lubricant (e.g., Vaseline) if friction is unavoidable	• Abnormal fluid collection within the layers of the skin • Exposure of underlying layers of skin	• Allow to heal on own to avoid risk of infection • If drained, apply anti-biotic ointment to avoid infection
Shin Splints	• Supportive, well cushioned shoes • Avoid running on hard surface • Avoid over-training	• Pain in the shin area • Should be evaluated by a medical professional to differentiate from stress fractures	• Relative Rest • Icing • Anti-inflammatory medication • Muscle strengthening • Supportive, well cushioned shoes • Gradual return to activity

Who's Your Doctor?

Each of us shoulders the responsibility of our own healthcare and quality of life. This can be a very complex and confusing task. It can be made easier for us if we know where to turn for information, services and support. Having access to professional health care practitioners is an important element in health maintenance. Selecting the right health care professional is an important decision that will benefit you for the rest of your life.

Today we have a lot of options for our medical care. We must have the knowledge to be proactive in making careful and educated decisions when it comes to our healthcare.

Conventional Western Medicine is based on scientifically proven methods, tests and trials. It is practiced by holders of M.D. (Doctor of Medicine) or D.O. (Doctor of Osteopathic Medicine) degrees and by their allied health professionals.

Health care practices and products that are not presently considered to be part of conventional medicine are called complimentary and alternative medicine (CAM). As we grow more frustrated with the limitations of conventional medicine millions of Americans are turning to CAM for their healing. CAM includes a wide range of healing philosophies, techniques and therapies. The practices of yoga, spirituality, relaxation, massage, acupuncture, homeopathy, chiropractic, herbalism, naturopathy and magnetic therapy are just a few. Each offers a different approach to treatment. However, we often don't know which approach to trust, or what accounts for their effectiveness, and many of our conventional medicine doctors are not able to tell us. The National Center for Complementary and Alternative Medicine (NCCAM) was established to examine new methods of healing.

A new model of medicine has emerged. It is a "healing partnership" that encourages teamwork to make patients well, and a personalized plan to keep them that way. This is called "Integrated Medicine", a collaborative, cross disciplinary approach to patient care. It is the integration of all the available resources to meet the full health care needs of the patient. Each of us is always changing and unique. We are a whole person, biological, psychological, and spiritual, in a total social and ecological environment and we will require different approaches to our health care needs.

Integrative medicine combines medical evaluations and consultation, workshops, health planning and coaching with many therapeutic services. Ideally, we will have informed doctors working with proactive patients who are both aware of the patient's individual needs and can draw from the many healing resources to establish an effective plan for lifelong health.

Selecting the right health care providers is an important decision that will benefit you for the rest of your life. The following resource guide will help you with this selection. Ultimately you are responsible for your own well-being. Your health should last a lifetime.

Types of Health Care Providers

Acupuncturists: Follow a healthcare practice that originated in traditional Chinese medicine. It involves inserting needles at specific points on the body, in the belief that this will help improve the flow of the body's energy and thereby help the body achieve and maintain health.

Anesthesiologist: A doctor who is primarily concerned with administering the various drugs that keep patients from feeling pain during surgery.

Cardiologist: A doctor that diagnoses and treats patients suffering from diseases of the heart, lungs, and blood vessels. They educate patients on preventing heart problems and living a heart-healthy lifestyle.

Chiropractor (DC): Believes that many diseases and ailments are related to misalignments of the vertebrae and emphasize the manipulation of the spinal column. Chiropractors use a type of hands on therapy called manipulation (adjustment) as their core clinical procedure.

Dentist: A practitioner who specializes in diseases of the teeth, gums, and oral cavity.

Oral/Maxillofacial Surgeon: A dentist that focuses on the diagnosis and surgical treatment of diseases, injuries and deformities of the teeth, mouth and jaw. An oral surgeon removes wisdom teeth, repairs broken jaws and treats a range of other conditions.

Orthodontist: A dentist who specializes in the correction and prevention of teeth irregularities.

Dermatologist: A doctor that treats disorders and diseases of the skin, ranging from warts to acne to skin cancers.

Endocrinologist: A doctor that is concerned with hormonal and metabolic disorders. They treat problems with the thyroid, pituitary and adrenal glands, as well as nutritional disorders, sexual disorders and problems such as diabetes and hypertension.

Gastroenterologist: A doctor that treats conditions of the digestive system. They diagnose and treat disorders of the stomach, intestines, bowels and other structures, such as the liver, gall bladder, pancreas and esophagus.

General Surgeon: Doctors that practice all types of common surgeries inv olving any part of the body.

Gynecologist/Obstetrician (OBGYN's): Is the field of medicine devoted to conditions specific to women. Obstetrics is the care of a woman during pregnancy and during and after childbirth. Gynecology is the study and care of the female reproductive system.

Hematologist: The medical specialist concerned with blood and the blood system. They treat blood diseases such as cancer, lymphoma, serious anemia and sickle cell disease.

Homeopaths: Practice an alternative medical system that was invented in Germany. Small, highly diluted quantities of medicinal substances are given to cure symptoms, when the same substances given at higher or more concentrated doses would actually cause those symptoms.

Immunologist: Doctors that are concerned with disorders of the immune system and allergies as well as the body's reaction to foreign substances. They treat hay fever, asthma, hives and other abnormal responses to allergens that range from dust and food to animals and chemicals.

Infectious disease: A doctor specializing in infectious diseases diagnoses and treats patients affected by illnesses ranging from pneumonia to salmonella to AIDS.

Licensed Clinical Social Worker (LCSWs): Are trained and state-licensed to provide various types of counseling and support.

Magnetic Therapist: Relies on magnetic energy to promote healing. This is an unconventional treatment.

Massage Therapist: Uses the techniques of rubbing or kneading body parts to treat ailments. Muscles and connective tissue are manipulated to enhance function of those tissues and promote relaxation and well-being.

Naturopaths: Follow an alternative medical system in which they work with natural healing forces within the body, with a goal of helping the body heal from disease and attain better health. Practices may include dietary modifications, massage, exercise, acupuncture, and various other interventions.

Neonatologist: A doctor devoted to the care and treatment of infants up to six weeks old. They treat all medical problems that can affect newborn babies.

Nephrologists: A doctor that treats kidney disorders, diabetes, renal failure and other illnesses. Treatments can range from dialysis to kidney transplants.

Neurologist: Doctors that treat diseases of the nervous system. A neurologist assists patients who have stroke complications, head injuries, epilepsy, Alzheimer's disease, and other afflictions of the brain and spinal cord.

Nurse Specialties

Certified Nurse Midwives (CNMs): Are RNs who have completed an advanced course of study and are certified by the American College of Nurse-Midwives. A midwife is trained to care for women during pregnancy, labor and the postnatal period, conduct normal deliveries, and to care for newborn babies under normal conditions.

Certified Registered Nurse Anesthetist (CRNAs): Are RNs with graduate training in the field of anesthesia.

Clinical Nurse Specialist (CNSs): Are RNs who have graduate training in a specialized clinical field, such as cardiac, psychiatric, or community health.

Licensed Practical Nurse (LPNs): Are state licensed caregivers who have been trained to care for the sick.

Nurse: A health care practitioner who assists in the diagnosis and treatment of health problems and provides many services to patients in a variety of settings.

Nurse Practitioners (NPs): Are (RNs) who have completed additional courses and specialized training in primary care. The profession includes family (FNP), pediatric (PNP), adult (ANP), and geriatric (GNP) specialties. In some states NPs can prescribe medications.

Registered Nurse (RNs): Has graduated from a nursing program and has passed state board examinations, and are licensed by the state.

Oncologists: Doctors that specialize in using various medications to treat and manage patients with cancer and some other diseases that resist treatment.

Ophthalmologist: A doctor devoted to the care of the eye and the treatment of diseases that eyes and vision. They diagnoses and treat abnormalities of the eye and perform surgery on the eye.

Opticians: Are not medical doctors. They make or sell corrective eyewear.

Optometrists: Are not medical doctors. They test vision and prescribe corrective lenses.

Orthopedic Surgeon: A doctor concerned with the prevention and correction of muscular or skeletal injuries and abnormalities. They treat complex conditions and injuries as well as broken bones, severe muscle sprains and knee and other joint injuries. They also perform joint replacements.

Osteopath (DO): Doctors of osteopathic medicine. Are medical practitioners, specializing in musculoskeletal problems. They are trained in conventional medicine and additional training in manipulative measures.

Otolaryngologist (ENT): A doctor that focuses on the ears, nose and throat. They diagnose and treat disorders from the shoulders up, with the exception of the eyes and brain. They may deal with hearing loss, tonsillitis and nasal obstructions.

Pediatrician: Doctors that care for infants, children and teenagers. They are often the first doctors children see.

Physician Assistant (PA): Is trained in the family practice model for a primary care role. They treat most standard cases of care.

Podiatrist (DPM): Attend colleges of podiatric medicine, and treat problems of the foot. They diagnosis and treat maladies of the foot and ankle by medical, surgical or mechanical means. Podiatrists with advanced training also do various types of foot surgery.

Primary Care Physician (MD): A doctor, who usually specializes in family practice or internal medicine. They are generalist and typically the patient's first contact for health care.

Psychiatrist: A doctor that diagnoses and treats mental, emotional and behavioral disorders. They prescribe appropriate medication and do therapy to treat a variety of conditions from depression to schizophrenia.

Psychologist: Are healthcare professionals with an advanced academic degree called a PhD. They deal with mental processes, both normal and abnormal and their effects upon human behavior. This involves the diagnosis, treatment, and prevention of mental and emotional disorders.

Pulmonologists: A doctor that treats diseases of the respiratory system These physicians treat pneumonia, bronchitis, emphysema, asthma, cancer and other disorders of the lungs and respiratory system.

Radiologists: A doctor that uses radioactive equipment, including x –ray machines and related procedures (ultrasound, MRI, CT), to diagnose and treat diseases and injuries.

Rheumatologist: A doctor that treats a range of conditions, from athletic injuries to arthritis, lupus and rheumatic fever.

Urologist: A doctor that treats disorders of the male and female urinary tracts and the male genital tract.

Useful Web Sites

National Institutes of Health (NIH)
   http://www.nih.gov
National Center for Complimentary and Alternative Medicine (NCCAM)
   http://altmed.od.nih.gov/nccam
Arthritis Foundation
   http://www.arthritis.org
American Chiropractic Association
   http://www.amerchiro.org
American Dental Association (ADA)
   http://www.ada.org
American Alliance for Health Physical Education, Recreation and Dance
   www.aahperd.org
American College of Sports Medicine
   www.acsm.org
American Medical Association
   http://www.ama-assn.org
American Nurses Association
   http://wwwnursingworld.org
American Holistic Medical Association (NHMA)
   http://www.ahmaholistic.com
National Center for Homeopathy (NCH)
   http://www.healthworld.com/nch
National Hospice Organization
   http://nho.org
Food and Drug Administration (FDA)
   http://www.fda.gov
American Psychiatric Association
   http://www.psych.org
American Psychological Association
   http://www.apa.org
National Institute of Mental Health
   www.nimh.nih.gov/
American Dietetic Association
   http://www.eatright.org
American Osteopathic Association
   http://www.am-osteo-assn.org
Consumer Product Safety Commission
   http://www.cpsc.gov
National Self-Help Clearinghouse (NSHC)
   http://selfhelpweb.org/
Sexual Information and Education Council of the U.S.(SIECUS)
   http://www.siecus.org
Centers for Disease Control and Prevention
   http://www.cdc.gov
American Cancer Society
   http://www.cancer.org

American Heart Association
      http://www.americanheart.org
National Runaway Switchboard
      http://nrs.crisisline.org/about.htm
Make-a-Wish Foundation of America (MAWFA)
      http://www.wish.org
National Wellness Institute
      www.nationalwellness.org
National Women's Health Network (NWHN)
      www.womenshealthnetwork.org

Review Questions

1. What is the difference between an acute injury and a chronic injury? Give the definition and some examples.
2. Describe how you can prevent heat exhaustion and heat stroke while exercising in warmer temperatures.
3. Relative rest for a chronic injury is an important part of treatment. Describe relative rest for plantar fasciitis in a runner, shoulder bursitis in a swimmer and tennis elbow in a tennis player.

References

Arnheim, D.D. & Prentice, W. E. (2003). *Principles of Athletic Training. Mosby Year Book,* 11th edition. St. Louis: McGraw-Hill.

Deles, Y.C.; Drez, D.; & Miller, M.D. (2003). *Orthopaedic Sports Medicine* 2nd Ed., Philadelphia, PA: W. B. Saunders Company.

Fu, F. & Slone, D.A. (2001). *Sports Injuries: Mechanism, Prevention, Treatment.* 2nd Ed. Philadelphia, PA: Lippincott, Williams & Wilkins.

Garrett, W.E.; Speer, K.P.; & Kirkendall, D.T., eds. (2000). *Principles and Practice of Orthopaedic Sports Medicine.* Philadelphia, PA: Lippincott Williams & Wilkins.

Garrett, W. E.; Kirkendall, D. T.; & Squire, D. L. eds. (2000). *Principles and Practice of Primary Care Sports Medicine.* Philadelphia, PA: Lippincott Williams & Wilkins.

Gordon, James (1996). *Manifesto For A New Medicine.* New York, NY: Addison–Wesley Publishing Co. Inc.

Hales, Dianne (2001). *An Invitation To Fitness & Wellness.* Belmont, CA: Wadsworth/Thomson.

Hoeger, Werner W.K. & Hoeger, Sharon A. (2006). *Principles & Labs For Fitness and Wellness.* 8th edition. Belmont, CA: Thomson/Wadsworth.

Krishnan, Anne (2007). *"Getting on the patients team."* Raleigh, NC: The News & Observer

Null, Gary (1999). *Get Healthy Now.* New York, NY: Seven Stories Press.

Souderi G.R. & McCann, P.D. (2005). *Sports Medicine: A Comprehensive Approach.* St. Louis, MO: Mosby.

Web Sites

http://www.swedish.org/body.cfm?id=984
http://adam.about.com/encycoopedia/001933.htm
http://www.bipolar.com/selecting_a_doctor.html
http://nccam.nih.gov/health/chiropractic/#homeo
www.acsm.org American College of Sports Medicine
www.journal.ajsm.org American Journal of Sports Medicine

www.sportsmed.org American Orthopaedic Society for Sports Medicine
http://www.healthfinder.gov U.S. Department of Health & Human Services
http://www.mayoclinic.com The Mayo Clinic – Tools for Healthier Lives
http://medlineplus.gov Medline Plus – Trusted Health Information For You
http://www.webmd.com/ WebMD – Better Information. Better Health

Cancer

Inquiries

1. What are some environmental or lifestyle factors that may potentially contribute toward a specific form of cancer in your own life?

   _____

   _____

   Responses of Others

   _____

   _____

2. Do you have any genetic predisposition toward a particular form of cancer? If so, what lifestyle changes are you making to decrease the risk?

   _____

   _____

   Responses of Others

   _____

   _____

Cancer is the leading cause of death in the United States and with an estimated 564,830 fatalities over 1,399,790 new cases in 2006. According to the Centers for Disease Control and Prevention (CDC) and the National Cancer Institute (NCI), about 10.5 million Americans were living with some form of invasive cancer in 2003. Additionally, the 2006 Annual Report to the Nation on the status of cancer indicated that cancer cases in women had increased by .3% since 1997. The number of new cancer diagnosis for Americans is expected to increase in the next 50 years from 1.3 million to 2.6 million. Once diagnosed, percent of cancer victims are expected to be alive five years later. This 5-year period, called relative survivability, include individuals living 5 years, cancer free, in remission or under treatment.

Causes of Cancer

The process to eradicate cancer has been slow. There is no single explanation for this phenomenon contributing factors include; aging population, tobacco use, high fat diet, pollution, lack of health insurance for the poor and underserved and delays in early diagnosis. Most researchers are optimistic that that new pharmacological agents and vaccines to prevent and treat cancer will be discovered. The term "cancer" is derived from the Latin word "crab" because it seemed to creep in all directions throughout the body. Cancer is not a disease but rather a large group of more than 100 different diseases characterized by uncontrolled growth and spread of abnormal cells. The causes of cancer are numerous and complex. The development of cancer, for each person, probably derives from many risk factors and cellular changes occurring over time.

Cancer occurs when a gene cell fails to do its job. The body depends on various cells to perform specific prescribed functions. When the cells fail to perform as prescribed, the body begins to deteriorate and the cells are no longer protected by the immune system. Cancer is therefore a disease caused by cell irregularity. When gene cells that control specialization, replication, DNA repair and tumor suppression of cells fail to do their job, they become cancer-causing genes known as oncogenes. Three possible causes of this gene alteration are genetic mutations, viral infections and carcinogens. Carcinogens are cancer causing agents such as tobacco, chemicals, toxic waste and polluted air and water.

The Cancerous Cell

Cancer cells (malignant tumors) differ from cancerous cells (benign tumors) in four ways:

1. Cancer cells have an infinite life expectancy compared to noncancerous cells. They have the capability to produce the enzyme, telomerase which blocks normal cell life expectancy and therefore do not die.
2. Cancer cells also lack the contact inhibition mechanism and therefore several cells can occupy one location as the same time.
3. Cancer cells do not have cellular cohesiveness and as such can not stick to their home-base. They have the ability to spread to distant locations through a process known as metastasis.
4. Cancer cells have the ability to demand extra blood supply from the circulatory system thus allowing them to metastasis through the routes. This is known as angiogenesis.

Types of Cancer

Cancers are named according to their point of origin in the body.

Carcinomas—these are found around the skin, nose mouth, throat, stomach, breasts, lungs, kidneys and other soft tissues. About 85% of all malignant tumors are carcinomas

Sarcomas—found around connective tissue such as bones, ligaments, cartilage and tendons. Only 2% of malignant tumors are sarcomas.

Leukemia—found in cells of the blood and blood-forming cells. Leukemia is evident in immature white blood cell formation.

Melanomas—comes from melanin-containing cells of the skin. More pronounced in individuals with prolonged sun-exposure. Recent increases in the form of cancer which can be very aggressive and deadly.

Lymphomas—arise from the lymphatic tissues and other immune system tissues. They include lymphosarcoma and Hodgkin's disease. They are characterized by irresistible abnormal white cell formation.

Hepatoma—found in cells of the liver although not directly linked to alcohol use. Hepatoma is often seen in individual with sclerotic livers.

Lung Cancer

Lung cancer is the leading cancer death in both men and women and only 15 percent of individuals diagnosed with the disease survive 5 years after diagnosis. This is due to the fact that by the time symptoms appear and diagnosis is made, it is often too late. Symptoms include persistent cough, blood-streaked sputum and chest pain.

Risk factors include:

genetic predisposition
cigarette smoking
environmental agents

Cigarette smoking is the single most preventable risk factor for lung cancer. According to National Cancer Institute, 87 percent of all reported lung cancer cases are from smokers. Among nonsmokers, radon is the most common agent known to cause lung cancer among nonsmokers.

Breast Cancer

Breast cancer is second to lung cancer as the second leading cause of cancer death in women. It is the most common cancer site in women. According to National Cancer Institute, one in eight women will develop breast cancer in their lifetime. In 2005, there was an estimated 211,240 new breast cancer cases and 40,410 deaths. Although breast cancer in men is less aggressive, 460 deaths in men in 2005 were due to breast cancer. Prevention includes (1) early detection through breast self-exams, clinical exams and mammography, (2) lifestyle changes (3) knowing one's family history as well as (4) prophylactic mastectomy. Prophylactic mastectomy is the surgical removal of the breasts to prevent breast cancer in women who are at high risk of developing the disease.

Risk factors include:

- First onset of menstrual cycle at an early age or late menopause
- Women who had no children or first child later in life or women who did not nurse.
- Women who used hormone replacement therapy (HRT).
- Women who consume high fat diets and lead sedentary lifestyles
- Women with a strong family history of breast cancer and who carry mutated tumor suppressor genes.

Breast Self-Examination (BSE) procedures should be performed after age 20 during the menstrual cycle or a day after. Proper techniques can be found at Memorial Sloan-Kettering Cancer Center at FMACROBUTTON HtmlResAnchor www.mskcc.org.

Mammography

The best tool for early detection of breast cancer is routine mammography. The American Cancer Society recommends that mammography begin at age 40. Women with a family history of breast cancer should begin at age 35 or younger. For women over 65, mammography screening frequency is a matter of individual recommendations from the physician.

Prostate Cancer

Prostate cancer is the most common cancer in men and is the second leading cancer death in men. In 2005, there were 232,090 new diagnosis and 30,500 deaths from prostate cancer. It is the leading cancer death in older men. The prostate which is located near the base of the penis and surrounds the bladder and urethra is a walnut-size gland whose function is to secrete some fluids responsible for sperm mortality. Risk factors for prostate cancer are not clear but include:

- Age—age is the most predictable risk factor. Majority of diagnosed cases are in men 65 years old and older.
- African-American men
- Family history
- Dietary fat and red meat
- Genetic mutation

Colon and Rectal

In 2005, colon and rectal cancer (colorectal) was the second leading cancer death in both in both men and women, claiming 56,290 lives. Two types of tumors carcinoma and lymphoma have been linked to colorectal cancer. With early detection, relative survivability rate from this cancer is as high as 90 percent. Risk factors include:

- Genetic predisposition
- High fat diets and red meat

Prevention includes:

- Removal of polyps
- Regular exercise
- Calcium intake
- Folic acid supplement
- Consistent low-dose aspirin (81 mg)
- Regular check ups-rectal exam after age 40 and stool blood test after age 50

Testicular Cancer

Testicular cancer is the least common form of cancer but is found in young men between the ages of 15 to 34. Testicular cancer awareness has greatly increased since Lance Armstrong and Scott Hamilton were diagnosed. Symptoms of include fatigue and abdominal discomfort. Testicular tumors often appear as a painless enlargement of the testis which can go undetected. Risk factors include:

- Undescended testicle at infancy
- Family history

- Environmental factors
- White males
- Mumps during childhood

Cervical Cancer

Four decades ago, cervical cancer was the leading cause of death for women in the United States. Although intervention strategies through Pap test have significantly lowered the mortality rates from cervical cancer the Human Papilloma Virus remains the most significant risk factor for cervical cancer. Epidemiological data from all over the world have shown the presence of HPV in 95 % of cervical cancer occurrences. Each year, there are about 13,000 diagnosed cervical cancer cases for American women. According to the National Cancer Institute, there were 9,710 new cases and 3,700 deaths have been reported in 2006. The National Cervical Cancer Public Education Campaign recommends that every sexually active woman be screened for cervical cancer. Exceptions apply only to those women who have had a total hysterectomy for reasons other than to treat cancer. A new vaccine Gerdasil by Merck, has been shown to be effective in preventing HPVs 16 and 18 strains that cause cervical cancer. Risk factors include:

- Early age of first intercourse
- Large number of sexual partners
- History of infertility
- Clinical presence of HPV
- Cigarette smoking
- Socio-ecomomic factors

Skin Cancer

Many forms of skin cancer will permanently disfigure or permanently change a person's appearance. Skin cancer is the most common type of all cancers. The sun is responsible for over one million cases of non-melanoma skin cancer found in the United States each year. According to the American Cancer Society there were 59,580 basal skin cancer cases in 2005, and 10,590 deaths. Eighty percent (80%) of reported deaths were from malignant melanoma. Risk factors include:

- Severe sunburn during childhood
- Fair complexion
- Family history
- Occupational exposure to coal, tar, pitch, creosote, arsenic compounds or radium

Prevention includes:

- use of sunscreen with a sun protection factor (SPF) of 15 or greater
- avoiding sun exposure between 11:00 A.M. to 2:00 P.M.

Skin cancer can be detected early, and both doctor and patient play a role in finding skin cancer. It is important for people to know what to look for. Moles often start as normal looking but change in size or color and acquire abnormal characteristics. A simple ABCD rule outlines the warning signs of melanoma:

- Asymmetry—one half of the mole does not match the other half
- Border irregularity—edges are uneven, notched or scalloped

- Color—pigmentation is not uniform. Melanoma may vary in color from tan to deeper brown, reddish black, black or deep bluish black
- Diameter—the diameter is greater those 6 millimeters (about the size of a pea)

The Seven Warning Signs of Cancer

The American Cancer Society has developed a list of seven early warning signs for cancer. The first letter in each word spells out the word CAUTION:

C Change in bowel or bladder habits
A A sore that does not heal
U Unusual bleeding or discharge
T Thickening or lump in breast or elsewhere
I Indigestion or difficulty in swallowing
O Obvious change in wart or mole
N Nagging cough or hoarseness

By paying close attention to these warning signs, the earlier cancer can be diagnosed, the better chance for treatment.

Guidelines for Preventing Cancer

1. Avoid tobacco use in all forms. Smoking is correlated to 85% of lung cancer cases.
2. Eat low fat, high fiber diet. Numerous studies have found links between diet and cancer. High risk diets are those that are high in calories and fat, and low in fiber.
3. Eat more cruciferous vegetables (cabbage, cauliflower, etc.) These help to reduce the risk of cancers such as colon cancer.
4. Avoid smoked or charcoal carcinogens.
5. Use alcohol in moderation. Heavy drinkers have increased oral and esophical cancers.
6. Avoid being overweight. Excess body weight and fat produces hormones that may promote cancerous growth.
7. Engage in aerobic exercise 4 times a week for at least 30 minutes.
8. Avoid sexually transmitted disease—STD viruses have been linked to cancers of the cervix and penis.
9. Reduce sunlight exposure.
    Avoid sunlamps
    Use sun block even when clouds are present
    Reapply sun block after swimming
10. Do regular self-exams for early detection
    Men—testicular cancer
    Women—breast cancer
11. Get a yearly check up by a health care provider

Review Questions

1. What is cancer?
2. What are the seven warning signs of cancer?
3. What are the three risk factors for cancer?
4. List five things you can do to prevent cancer.
5. List four lifestyle factors for cancer.

References

Dailard, C. (2003). HPV in the US and Developing Nations. A problem of Public Health or Politics? The Guttmar Report, 6, 3, 1–6.

Donatelle, R.J. (2003). *Health: the Basics* (5th ed.). San Francisco, CA: Benjamin Cummings.

Eldin, G. & Golanty, E. (1992). *Health & Wellness.* (4th Ed.). Boston, MA: Jones and Bartlett Publishers.

Hahn, D. B., Payne, W. A. & Lucus, E. B. (2006). *Focus on Health,* (8th. Ed.) New York, NY: McGraw-Hill.

Jay, N. & Moscicki, A-B., (2000). "Human Papilloma Virus Infection in Women." In: Marlene Goldman & Maureen Hatch, eds. Women and Health, Academic Press.

Williams, B.K. & Knight, S.M. (1994). *Healthy for Life: Wellness and the Art of Living.* Belmont, CA: Brook/Cole Publishing.

Web Sites

www.cancer.org American Cancer Society

www.aicr.org American Institute for Cancer Research

www.nci.nih.gov National Cancer Institute

www.cdc.gov The Center for Disease Control and Prevention

www.yourdiseaserisk.harvard.edu Harvard Center For Cancer Prevention

www.drday.com Dr. Lorraine Day "Cancer Does Not Scare Me Anymore"

www.healthypeople.gov Healthy People 2010 Objectives

www.mskcc.org Memorial Sloan-Kettering Cancer Center

www.gardasil.com Merck

Addictive Behaviors

Inquires

1. Without stating specifically, do you or someone close to you have an addiction that is of concern? Are you aware of resources that deal with this addictive behavior? What steps might you take to improve this situation for yourself or the other individual?

_____

_____

_____

_____

_____

Responses of Others

_____

_____

2. Does an individual have a right to be self-destructive with his/her own personal health behavior?

_____

_____

Responses of Others

_____

_____

Millions of Americans struggle with compulsive and harmful behaviors collectively known as addictions. Examples of these include: alcohol, tobacco, various forms of legal and illegal drugs, food, exercise, gambling, work, over spending and unsafe sex.

Addiction can be defined as an unhealthy, potentially harmful, compulsive interaction with an activity or substance. Pleasure and/or sense of normalcy is obtained by the person who is engaged in the addictive behavior. Most researchers agree that addictions are a combination of psychological and physiological dependence. These two states are interconnected in that most addictions have components of both. Researchers theorize that some people have insufficient chemicals in the brain that are correlated to pleasure, thus they seek out activities (exercise) or chemicals (alcohol/nicotine) that produce pleasurable feelings and reduce discomfort. These pleasurable experiences become a focal point in their lives. Psychological dependence refers to a strong desire to repeat the use of a chemical or activity based one motional/mental reasons such as feelings of pleasure, relief of tension, and enhancement of self-esteem. Physiological dependence refers to state of functional adaptation of the brain's nerves to a substance or activity that produces a chemical in which the presence of the chemical becomes normal and necessary. Abstaining from the chemical or physical activity will produce withdrawal symptoms both physical and psychological. Example of these symptoms include anxiety, irritability and distress.

Addictions may be characterized by four common symptoms:

1. Compulsion: which includes obsession (excessive preoccupation with an activity or substance) and an intense need to perform or engage in the activity or substance.
2. Loss of control: inability to control urges or desires to use a substance or perform a behavior.
3. Negative consequences: person will suffer from health problems, legal trouble, relationship conflicts and so on.
4. Denial: inability to perceive that behavior/substance is destructive to oneself. The family may also be in denial, which enables the addicted person to continue in the behavior/substance.

The addiction process is one that evolves over time. Addictions have a powerful hold on people's lives. Fortunately there are a variety of self-help programs, 12-step programs and qualified therapists to help people regain control over their own lives.

Review Questions

1. What are the four common symptoms of addictive behaviors?

References

Donatell, R.J. & Davis, L.G. (1966). *Access to Health* (4th ed.). Needham Heights, MA: Allyn and Bacon.

Hahn, D.B. & Payne, W.A. (2001). *Focus on Health* (5th ed.). New York, NY: McGraw Hill.

Pinger, R.R.; Payne, W.A.; & Hahn, E.J. (1995). *Drugs: Issues For Today* (2nd ed.). St. Louis, MO: Mosby Year Book.

Sexually Transmitted Infections (STI)

Inquiries

1. Do you think it should be a criminal act if someone knowingly withholds information concerning a sexually transmitted disease that he/she has and then transmits that STD to a sexual partner?

_____

_____

Responses of Others

_____

_____

2. Discuss when sex education should begin in grades 1 through 12 and what the depth of the content should be.

_____

_____

Responses of Others

_____

_____

Hot Line: 800–227–8922

The continual rise of STD's is the result of many factors. There is a rise in sexual activity with many individuals having multiple partners. Due to the increased use of birth control pills, the use of spermicides and condoms has decreased. Many of the STD diseases do not produce obvious symptoms, so many people are unaware that they have an STD. Feelings of guilt, embarrassment and denial prevent many people from seeking adequate treatment.

Chlamydia

In the 1980's, Chlamydia was recognized as a wide spread STI. Chlamydia is caused by bacterial infection, it invades the cells it attacks and multiplies within them like a virus. It is among the most prevalent and most damaging of STIs. The Center for Disease Control (CDC) estimates 3 million infections per year in the United States.

Transmission is primarily through sexual contact. It may be spread by fingers from one body site to another, such as genitals to eyes. Genital chlamydia infection in females can include infections of lower reproductive tract (urethritis or cervicitis) and infections of upper reproductive tract (Pelvic inflammatory disease). Pelvic inflammatory disease (PID) is an infection of the lining of uterus, fallopian tubes and possibly the ovaries and adjacent abdominal structures. Chlamydia may account for as many as a half of a million annual U.S. cases of PID.

Around 70% of infected people have no early symptoms. Symptoms occur 1 to 3 weeks after exposure. Most women with lower reproductive tract chlamydia infections have few or no symptoms. In men, chlamydia is estimated to be the cause of half of the cases of epididymitis and nongonococcal urethritis.

Gonorrhea (Clap):

There are 650,000 reported cases each year and an estimated 1 million overall including unreported cases in the United States. Gonorrhea is caused by a bacterial infection. It grows in mucous membranes. Outside the body, it dies in a few seconds. The bacteria survives in warm mucous membranes of the genitals, anus and throat. It is transmitted by sexual contact, vaginal intercourse, oral sex and anal sex.

Early symptoms in the male appear within 1 to 5 days after contact. However, symptoms may show up as late as 2 weeks later, or, in a small percentage of cases, not at all. Early symptoms sometimes clear up on their own without treatment; however, the bacteria often moves on to other organs such as prostate, bladder, kidneys, and testicles. It may move down the vas deferens, inflaming the epididymis and causing scar tissue, which can block the flow of sperm.

As many as 80% of females have no early symptoms and are unaware of the infection. The primary site of infection is the cervix, which becomes inflamed without observable symptoms. A green or yellowish discharge usually results, and may go undetected. There is an increased risk of PID as the bacteria moves upward.

Syphilis

There are 20,000 reported cases each year in the U.S. Some STD specialists speculate that as many as nine cases go unreported for each one recorded. Syphilis is an STI caused by thin, corkscrew-like bacterium (treponema pallidum-spirochete). It is transmitted from open lesions to mucous membranes or skin abrasions of partners through penilevaginal, oral-genital or genital-anal contact. There are four classes of syphilis, primary, secondary, latent, and tiertiary.

1. Primary
   Approximately 10 to 90 days (average 21 days) after exposure a chancre appears at site where spirochete enters the body. In women, the sore appears on the inner wall of the vagina, cervix or on labia. In men, it most often appears on the glans of penis, penile shaft or scrotum. It often goes undiscovered on internal structures. The chancre generally heals without treatment in 4 to 6 weeks.
2. Secondary
   A skin rash appears usually on the palms of hands and the soles of feet. Raised bumps develop that have a

rubbery, hard consistency that typically does not hurt or itch. Other symptoms are fever, swollen lymph glands, fatigue, weight loss and sores. Symptoms subside within a few weeks and enter the next stage.

3. Latent
   This stage can last for several years. More than half of untreated syphilis victims remain in the latent stage for the rest of their lives. There may be no observable symptoms. Organisms may continue to multiply, preparing for final stage.

4. Tertiary
   The final stage can be severe, resulting in death. Bacteria multiply and attack various organs and tissues. This stage can occur anywhere from 3 to 40 years after infection and may cause heart failure, blindness, ruptured blood vessels, paralysis, liver damage,or severe mental disturbances.

Herpes

Approximately 100 million Americans have oral herpes and 50 million have genital herpes. Herpes is caused by herpes simplex virus (HSV). A virus is an organism that invades, reproduces and lives within a cell. The most common are HSV-1 (usually sores appear on/around mouth and lips) and HSV-2 (usually sores appear on/around genital areas). About 20% of genital herpes is linked to HSV-1. There are an estimated 1 million new cases of genital herpes each year. Transmission of genital herpes occurs primarily by penile-vaginal, oral-genital, or genital-anal contact. Transmission of oral herpes occurs from kissing.

When sores are present, the person is highly contagious. The virus can be spread from one part of body to another by touching a sore and then scratching elsewhere, a process known as autinoculation. Herpes in the eyes, keratitis, can damage the cornea.Not all individuals experience recognizable symptoms. In women, symptoms occur on the labia, inner walls of the vagina and the cervix. In men, symptoms occur on the glans or the shaft of the penis. Red bumps develop into tiny, painful blisters filled with a clear fluid containing virus particles. The body attacks the virus with white blood cells, causing blisters to become filled with pus. Blisters rupture to form wet, painful, open sores surrounded by a red ring. Open sores form a crust and then begin to heal, which may take up to two weeks. Avoid contact for 10 days after the sores have healed. Sores on cervix take much longer to heal. Infection may take up to 4 weeks to heal.

Many individuals have periodic flare-ups. In cases of HSV-2, 7 to 30% of patients have at least one recurrence. Studies show that the more extensive the primary attack, the greater the chance of recurrence. Of those who experience recurrence, as many as 75% experience prodromal symptoms (itching, burning, throbbing, tingling at sites, sometimes pain in legs, thighs groin or buttocks) which give advance warning of eruption. An individual's infectiousness increases during this stage. Factors that may trigger reactivation of herpes include emotional stress which can weaken the immune system, sunburn, cold, poor nutrition and being over-tired or exhausted.

HPV (Human Papillomavirus) or Genital Warts

In 1992, HPV became the most common viral STI in the U.S. The incidence is rapidly increasing in both sexes with ~ 35 million reported cases. 1–5 million new cases happen each year. There are 60 types, of which 7 cause outgrowth of warts. HPV is transmitted by skin to skin contact, where one individuals infects the other by transmitting the virus. The incubation period ranges from 3 weeks to 3 months. In many cases, the warts are not largely visible and may go undetected in the early stages. In moist areas, they are pink/red and soft with a cauliflower-like appearance. In dry areas, they are generally hard and yellow-gray. Some people carry the virus without developing any symptoms. There is a strong association between HPV and cancers of the cervix, vagina, vulva, penis and anus.

HIV: Human Immunodeficiency Virus

In the U.S., there are up to 1 million people with HIV and 40,000 new cases of HIV each year. Worldwide, there are 33 million people infected with HIV, with over 3 million new infections each year. HIV causes AIDS. It took 8 years to record the first 100,000 AIDS cases; just 2 years for the next 100,000 cases.

STD	Symptoms	Diagnosis	Treatment
Chlamydia	**Females:** • Mild irritation • Itching of genital tissues • Burning during urination • Slight discharge *PID symptoms* • Disrupted menstrual periods • Pain in the lower abdomen • Elevated temperature • Nausea • Vomiting • Ectopic pregnancy may also occur **Males:** • Burning sensation during urination and discharge of pus • Sensation of heaviness in the affected testicle • Inflammation of scrotal skin • Formation of small area of hard painful swelling of the testicle	1. Obtain urethral or cervical discharge, grow a culture and examine the culture. 2. A urine test that detects bacterial DNA in the urine.	Treated and cured with a week of antibiotic drugs such as erythromycin and doxycycline. Penicillin is not effective.
Gonorrhea (Clap)	• Foul-smelling yellowish-green, cloudy discharge from the penis • Burning sensations during urination	1. A smear is made of the discharge and examined microscopically. 2. A culture is grown and then examined. 3. An application of an enzyme-sensitive immunoassay can detect gonorrhea.	Penicillin used to be the cure-all; however, there are now penicillin-resistant strains, so patients may use ceftriaxone, azithromycin and doxycycline.
Herpes	• Small painful, red bumps which usually appear between 2 and 12 days after sexual contact	1. Direct observation 2. Cultures of virus grown in lab	Antiviral drugs, such as acyclovir, to reduce discomfort and speed healing during the initial outbreak. Use of valacylcloir has been shown to both suppress and reduce duration or outbreaks.
Syphilis	1. **Primary** • Painless sore ("chancre") ~ 10 to 90 days after exposure, at site where spirochete enters the body. • 95% of chancres are on the genitals; others occur in the mouth, lips, tongue, rectum or anus. 2. **Secondary** • Skin rash on hands and feet. • Raised bumps with rubbery, hard consistency (typically, does not hurt or itch). • Fever, swollen lymph glands, fatigue, weight loss and sores. 3. **Latent** • May be no observable symptoms. 4. **Tertiary** Severe, may result in death.	1. Blood tests 2. Microscopic examination of fluid from chancre.	Primary and secondary syphilis treated with a single intramuscular injection of penicillin. If the patient is allergic, then tetracycline erythromycin can be prescribed. Latent and tertiary syphilis requires larger doses of antibiotics over a period of several weeks.

STD	Symptoms	Diagnosis	Treatment
HPV (Human Papilloma virus) or Genital Warts	**Females:** • warts appear at the bottom part of vaginal opening, perineum, labia, inner walls of vagina and cervix. **Males:** • warts commonly occur on glans, foreskin and shaft of penis.	1. Observation 2. Tissue biopsy	Remove by laser. Treat with acid. Topical applications (podophyllin). Freeze with liquid nitrogen. Surgical removal. The virus remains in the body and warts can often reappear.

The most common fluids involved in the transmission of the HIV are blood, semen and vaginal secretions. The virus can be transmitted in the womb and through breast milk.HIV is found in saliva, tears, urine and feces, but the possibility of transmission from this fluids has been shown to be unlikely.

Routes of HIV infection:

1. Vaginal or anal intercourse
2. Oral-genital sex
3. Contact with infected semen or vaginal fluids
4. Infected organ transplant
5. Use of contaminated needles
6. Transfer from mother to child

HIV's Impact upon the Immune System:

HIV is a retrovirus which consists of a protein shell surrounding the genetic material RNA. HIV attaches to T-lymphocytes known as CD4s, a type of white blood cell, and injects its RNA into the CD4 cell. RNA is then converted into DNA by an enzyme called reverse transcriptase. The HIV DNA hijacks the CD4's DNA, causing the cell to become a viral factory. Numerous viral particles are produced, and then they break through the CD4 membrane, causing cellular death, and go on to invade other CD4 cells. Over time, this action suppresses the immune system, leaving the individual vulnerable to other infectious agents.

HIV Infection Stages:

There are four stages of HIV infection. The duration of these stages varies according to the person's health.

1. Primary HIV disease occurs soon after being infected with HIV, some people experience a fever, swollen glands and fatigue. They may think they have the flu. As the immune system charges into action, these symptoms usually subside within a couple of weeks.
2. Chronic asymptomatic disease is a decline in the immune cells with no specific disease symptoms.
3. Chronic symptomatic disease is a major depletion of immune cells, leaving the body vulnerable to opportunistic infections. One common infection is a yeast infection of the mouth called thrush. Other symptoms during this stage are fevers, diarrhea, night sweats and weight loss.
4. AIDS: diagnosis is made after one or more of 26 diseases has appeared. An example is pnuemocystis carinii which is pneumonia caused by a proliferation of a fungus due to a suppressed immune system.

HIV Testing:

When someone becomes infected with HIV, the body begins to produce antibodies in an attempt to destroy the virus. Antibodies to the virus are what HIV tests are trying to detect. Generally antibodies show up anywhere from 3 to 6 months after infection. Thus, a person may be advised to wait 3 to 6 months after their last suspected infection incident. The local health department can administer a HIV test.

Review Questions

1. Why are STDs increasing?
2. What is HIV and its symptoms?
3. What is AIDS?
4. List how HIV can be prevented.

References

Kelly, G.F. (2001). *Sexuality Today: The Human Perspective* (7th ed.). New York, NY: McGraw-Hill.

Kelly, G.F. (2004). *Sexuality Today: The Human Perspective* (updated 7th ed.). New York, NY: McGraw-Hill.

Greenberg, J.S.; Bruess, C.E.; & Haffner, D.W. (2004). *Exploring the Dimensions of Human Sexuality* (2nd ed.). Sudbury, MA: Jones and Bartlett.

Web Sites

www.ashastd.org American Social Health Association
www.cdc.gov.nchstp/od/nchstp CDC Center for STD Prevention
www.cdcpin.org Prevention Information Network
AIDS: Acquired Immunodeficiency Syndrome
Hotline: 800-342-AIDS (2437)
Clearinghouse: www.cdc.gov

SECTION 4

Appendices

Adapted Physical Education

Adapted Physical Education offers education, information, and training for those individuals that require modifications for physical activity. An individual's health condition may require physical education in an Adapted Physical Education class or he/she may participate in the regular physical education classes with minor modifications.

Health Conditions That Might Warrant Adapted Physical Education

1. Anemia
2. Arthritis
3. Asthma
4. Cardiovascular problems
5. Cystic fibrosis
6. Diabetes
7. Epilepsy
8. Kidney disorders
9. Muscular disorders
10. Obesity
11. Paralysis

Medication Considerations

Please inform your physical education instructor if you are taking medication for which side effects may be exacerbated due to physical activity.

- Diuretics—Diuretics may be used to manage obesity, heart disease, high blood pressure and other conditions. When engaged in vigorous exercise or exercise in hot, humid conditions, the exerciser should consumer water frequently. Diuretics may cause hypovolemia (excessive fluid loss) and hypokalemia (diminished blood volume, causing serious depletion of potassium). Both of these are life threatening. **Watch for these signs:** dizziness, weakness and muscle cramps.
- Seizure Drugs—These drugs may cause poor reaction time, lack of coordination and attention problems.

- Asthma—Drugs for asthma typically dilate the bronchial tubes and may create an increase in heart rate. Be sure to monitor your heart rate frequently if you use drugs to treat asthma.
- Blood pressure drugs—Drugs that are used to decrease blood pressure may also mask the intensity of physical activity. Therefore, the usual methods of monitoring heart rate (ie., counting the pulse or using a heart rate monitor) may be an inaccurate measure of the intensity of the workout. If you take alpha- and/or beta-blocker drugs, use the Rating of Perceived Exertion Scale or "Talk Test" to monitor your heart rate.
- Drugs for Attention Deficit Hyperactivity Disorder (ADHD) may have the following adverse side effects, which could affect physical fitness training: anorexia, nausea, dizziness, pulse changes (up or down), tachycardia and cardiac arrhythmia.

Exercise Guidelines

Anemia

- Individuals with mild to moderate anemia do not need restrictions for physical activity.
- Anaerobic activities are best for individuals with anemia.
- Aerobic activities tend to cause undue fatigue (because of the lowered blood oxygen levels).
- Severe anemia may cause enlargement of the liver or spleen and contraindicates all but very mild exercise.

Arthritis

- Rheumatoid arthritis is generally most problematic early in the day and osteoarthritis typically becomes more painful as the day goes on. Select physical activity during the time of day that you are most pain free.
- Movement and activity is essential because sitting for long periods of times puts stress on the joints.
- Three types of physical training are recommended: range of motion, aerobic exercise and strength training.
- Prior to exercise use heat or ice as needed and/or recommended by your physician.
- Warm up gradually with low intensity exercise.
- Swimming is an excellent non-weight bearing activity that can also increase flexibility; other non-weight bearing activities such as bicycling and rowing are also recommended.
- Weight lifting is recommended in order to increase lean tissue and maintain stability in the joints.

Asthma

- A gradual aerobic warm-up helps the airways adjust slowly to the increased demand placed on them.
- Anaerobic activity (short bursts of energy/speed) workouts may be preferable to an aerobic workout.
- Exercising in a warm, humid environment is recommended (swimming is an excellent choice) unless you experience adverse reactions to mold or chlorine.
- If exercising outdoors, avoid those time periods when pollen counts are high.
- Monitor your exercise intensity with the "talk test."

Cardiovascular Problems

- The individual with a cardiovascular problem is encouraged to consider the ABCDEF plan, taking into account severity and/or frequency of symptoms, when exercising:
  - Angina
  - Breathing difficulty
  - Color change, bluish or pale
  - Dizziness
  - Edema, fluid retention and swelling of extremities
  - Fatigue

Cystic Fibrosis

- Scuba diving in contraindicated.
- If cystic fibrosis is severe, the individual may be at risk for an increased loss of fluid during exercise.
- A heart rate monitor is recommended so that the individual exercises within a specified heart rate range.

Diabetes

- Be sure to have a detailed medical exam before beginning any exercise program.
- Individuals with Type 1 diabetes should avoid exercise if their fasting glucose levels are more than 250 mg/dl and ketosis is present or if their glucose levels are over 300.
- Monitor blood glucose before and after exercise and eat enough carbohydrates to avoid hypoglycemia.
- Follow the ACSM guidelines for frequency, intensity and duration of aerobic exercise in order to maintain body weight and body composition.

Epilepsy

- There is no evidence that intense physical activity increases the likelihood of a seizure.
- If you have been experiencing frequent seizures, be sure to exercise with a partner, and if you are weight lifting, avoid doing free weight lifts in which the motion is to take the weight over your head or chest.
- Always swim with a partner.
- Gymnastics requires a spotter when on the high bar, balance beam, parallel bars and trampoline.
- Boxing is contraindicated and "heading" the ball in soccer is discouraged.

Kidney Disorders

- For first time exercisers, begin with a graduated exercise program. Exercise aerobically for 10 minutes (if you are an individual on dialysis, be sure to exercise on non-dialysis days), and then increase the length of exercise by one to three minutes per week.
- Participate in weight training—keep a journal to monitor your progress and keep track of becoming fatigued.
- If you are on dialysis, be sure to monitor your fluid intake (liquids and in foods you eat), and adjust your workout accordingly (ie., level of intensity, and whether you work out inside or outside) if excess fluid is building up in your body.

Muscular Disorders

- The goal for the individual with a muscular disorder is to maintain function for as long as possible. Therefore avoid activities that create fatigue or pain.
- Allow yourself to have frequent rest breaks during activity. Interval training is preferred to continuous aerobic activity.
- Be flexible with your workout schedule so that you can workout when you feel most rested.

Obesity

- The individual that is obese should select non-weight bearing activities for aerobic activities, and the activity should be strenuous enough to elevate the heart rate to the target heart rate range.
- The individual should participate in weight training to build lean tissue, which in turn will increase his/her metabolism.
- Be sure to acclimate to hot, humid weather and to drink plenty of water before, during and after activity.
- Wear light, loose-fitting clothing.

Paralysis

- A number of assistive devices are available so that the person with paralysis can participate as fully as possible in physical fitness classes.
- When the lower body is affected, the individual can utilize upper body weights and an arm ergometer. The exercising heart rate will generally be 10–20 beats per minute less than for an exercise that works the large muscles of the body; therefore, monitor the heart rate using the rating of perceived exertion (RPE).
- Exercising in water is excellent for individuals with paralysis or limited use of the limb(s).

References

Sherrill, C. (2003). *Adapted Physical Activity, Recreation, and Sport* (6th ed.). Boston, MA: McGraw-Hill.

Auxter, D.; Pyfer, J.; & Huettig, C. (1997). *Principles and Methods of Adapted Physical Education and Recreation* (8th ed.). St. Louis, MO: Mosby-Year Book.

Web Sites

www.healthysource.com/ritalin.html (Ritalin)
www.mendosa.com (diabetes information)
www.mckinley.uiuc.edu (ACSM guideline for special populations)
www.mobictablet.com (arthritis)

Fitness Tests: Run, Walk, and Swim

1.5 Mile Run Test

Fitness Category		Age (years)					
		13–19	20–29	30–39	40–49	50–59	60+
I. Very poor	(men)	>15:31*	>16:01	>16:31	>17:31	>19:01	>20:01
	(women)	>18:31	>19:01	>19:31	>20:01	>20:31	>21:01
II. Poor	(men)	12:11–15:30	14:01–16:00	14:44–16:30	15:36–17:30	17:01–19:00	19:01–20:00
	(women)	16:55–18:30	18:31–19:00	19:01–19:30	19:01–20:00	20:01–20:30	21:00–21:31
III. Fair	(men)	10:49–12:10	12:01–14:00	12:31–14:45	13:01–15:35	14:31–17:00	16:16–19:00
	(women)	14:31–16:54	15:55–18:30	16:31–19:00	17:31–19:30	19:01–20:00	19:31–20:30
IV. Good	(men)	9:41–10:48	10:46–12:00	11:01–12:30	11:31–13:00	12:31–14:30	14:00–16:15
	(women)	12:30–14:30	13:31–15:54	14:31–16:30	15:56–17:30	16:31–19:00	17:31–19:30
V. Excellent	(men)	8:37–9:40	9:45–10:45	10:00–11:00	10:30–11:30	11:00–12:30	11:15–13:59
	(women)	11:50–12:29	12:30–13:30	13:00–14:30	13:45–15:55	14:30–16:30	16:30–17:30
VI. Superior	(men)	<8:37	<9:45	<10:00	<10:30	<11:00	<11:15
	(women)	<11:50	<12:30	<13:00	<13:45	<14:30	<16:30

< Means "less than"; > means "more than."

"1.5 mile run tests," from *The Aerobics Program for Total Well Being* by Kenneth H. Copper M.D., M.P.H. Copyright © 1982 by Kenneth H. Copper.

Rockport Fitness Walking Test

The Rockport Walking Institute has developed a walking test to assess cardiorespiratory fitness for men and women ages 20–69.

1. Find a 1-mile course that is flat, uninterrupted, and correctly measured. A quarter-mile track is preferable.
2. Walk 1 mile as quickly and comfortably as possible.
3. Immediately take a heart rate by counting your pulse for 15 seconds and multiplying that number by four (to get your heart for one minute).
4. Record your score and rating.

   Use the Rockport relative fitness charts to classify your cardiorespiratory fitness. The walking time and corresponding postexercise heart rate are located on the appropriate chart for your age and gender. These charts are based on body weights of 125 lb. for women and 170 lb. for men. If you weigh substantially more than this value, your cardiorespiratory fitness level will be overestimated.

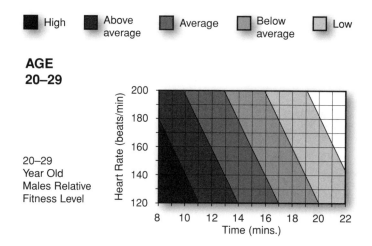

AGE 20–29

20–29 Year Old Males Relative Fitness Level

20–29 Year Old Females Relative Fitness Level

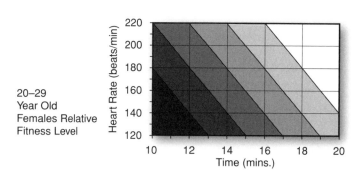

AGE 30–39

30–39 Year Old Males Relative Fitness Level

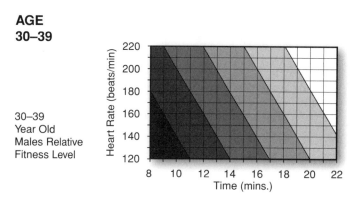

30–39 Year Old Females Relative Fitness Level

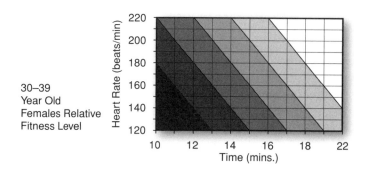

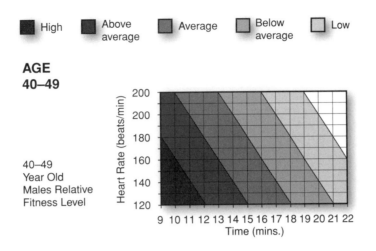

**AGE
40–49**

40–49
Year Old
Males Relative
Fitness Level

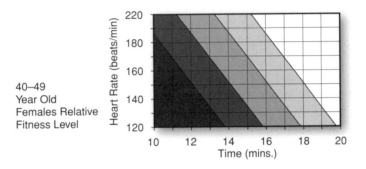

40–49
Year Old
Females Relative
Fitness Level

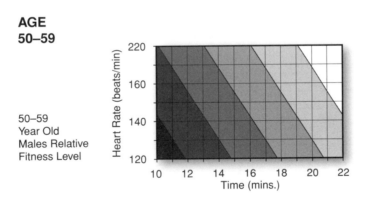

**AGE
50–59**

50–59
Year Old
Males Relative
Fitness Level

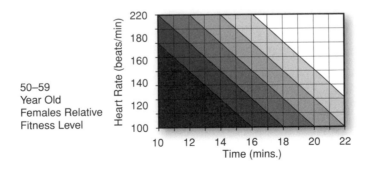

50–59
Year Old
Females Relative
Fitness Level

Swim Test

450 Yard Fitness Swim Classifications

Time	Classification	Distance
5:00	SUPERIOR	450 yds
5:10		
5:30		
5:40		
5:55		
6:10		
6:20		
6:29		
6:30	EXCELLENT	450 yds
6:40		
6:50		
7:00		
7:10		
7:15		
7:24		
7:25	GOOD	450 yds
7:35		
7:45		
7:55		
8:10		
8:20		
8:29		
8:30	AVERAGE	450 yds
8:40		
8:45		
8:50		
9:05		
9:15		
9:24		
9:25	POOR	450 yds
9:35		
9:45		
9:55		
10:15		
10:20		
>10:20	VERY POOR	450 yds

From NCSU PE Dept.

Estimating Energy Expenditure

STEP 1: Convert your weight to kilograms (kg)

Your weight in pounds _____ ÷ 2.2 = _____ kg

STEP 2: Determine the MET value of your activity

Activity: _____

METS: _____ (see following pages)

Time spent doing activity (hours*): _____ hours

Time must be reported in hours, example 15 minutes (15 min/60 min) = .25 hours

STEP 3: Plugging in the values

Weight (kg) × MET value × time (hours) = calories expended

_____ × _____ × _____ = _____

Think of the activities you do every day. Can you increase the intensity (MET level) of those activities? See the chart below for some examples.

Activity	METS
HOME ACTIVITIES	
Carpet sweeping, sweeping floors	3.3
Cleaning, heavy or major (eg., wash car, wash windows, clean garage) vigorous effort	3.0
Mopping	3.5
Multiple household tasks, light to vigorous	2.5–4
Cleaning, light (dusting, straightening up, changing linen, carrying out trash)	2.5
Wash dishes—standing or in general (not broken into stand/walk components); clearing dishes from table—walking	2.3–2.5
Vacuuming	3.5
Cooking, food preparation, serving	2–2.5
Putting away groceries (eg., carrying groceries, shopping without a grocery cart, carrying packages)	2.5
Carrying groceries upstairs	7.5
Ironing	2.3
Moving furniture and household items, carrying boxes	6.0
Scrubbing floors, on hands and knees, scrubbing bathroom, bathtub	3.8
Sweeping garage sidewalk or outside of house	4.0
Standing—packing, unpacking boxes, occasional lifting of household items (light/moderate effect)	3.5
Watering plants	2.5
Moving household items upstairs, carrying boxes or furniture	9.0
Walk/run—playing with children—light to vigorous	2.5–5
Walk/run, playing with animals, light to vigorous	2.5–5
Standing—bathing dog	3.5
HOME REPAIR	
Automobile body work, repair	3–4
Carpentry	3–7.5
Caulking	4.5–5
Cleaning gutters	5.0
Hanging storm windows	5.0
Laying or removing carpet, tile or linoleum	4.5
Painting	3–5.0
Roofing	6.0
LAWN AND GARDEN	
Carrying, loading or staking wood, loading/unloading or carrying lumber	5.0
Clearing land, hauling branches, wheelbarrow chores	5.0
Digging, filling garden, composting	5.0
Gardening with heavy power tools, tilling a garden, chain saw	6.0
Moving lawn, general	5.5
Mowing lawn, riding mower	2.5
Mowing lawn, walking, hand mower	6.0
Mowing lawn, walking, power mower	5.5
Operating snow blower, walking	4.5
Planting seedlings, shrubs, trees	4.5
Raking lawn	4.3
Raking roof with snow rake	4.0
Sacking grass, leaves	4.0
Shoveling snow by hand	6.0
Trimming shrubs or trees, using manual cutter or power cutter, using leaf blower	3.5–4.51
Watering lawn or garden, standing or walking	1.5
Weeding, cultivating garden	4.5

Activity	METS
SELF CARE	
Standing, getting ready for bed, in general	2.0
Sitting on toilet	1.0
Bathing (sitting)	1.5
Dressing, undressing (standing, sitting)	2.0
Eating (sitting)	1.5
Talking and eating	1.5–2
Grooming (washing, shaving, brushing teeth)	2.0
Hairstyling	2.5
Showering, toweling off, standing	2.0
SEXUAL ACTIVITY	
Passive to active	1–1.5
OCCUPATION	
Baker	2.5–4
Carrying heavy loads, such as bricks	8.0
Carrying moderate loads up stairs, moving boxes (16–40 pounds)	8.0
Construction, outside, remodeling	5.5
Fire fighter, general	8–12
Forestry, ax chopping, slow	4–11
Horse grooming	6.0
Masseur, masseuse, standing	4.0
Moving, pushing heavy objects, 75 lbs or more (desks, moving van work)	7.5
Shoveling, digging ditches	6–9
Walking downstairs or standing, carrying objects about 25–74 lbs	5–7.5
Walking or walking downstairs or standing, carrying objects about 75 to 100 lbs or over	7.5–8.5
Driving	2.0
Playing Music	1.8–4
FISHING AND HUNTING	
Digging worms with shovel	4.0
Fishing from river bank and walking	4.0
Fishing from boat, sitting	2.5
Fishing from river bank, standing	3.5
Fishing in stream in waders	6.0
Ice Fishing, sitting	2.0
Hunting, bow and arrow or crossbow, trap shooting, pistol shooting, etc.	2.5–6
DANCING	
Aerobic, low impact, high impact	5–7
Aerobic step, with 6–8 inch step	8.5
Aerobic step, with 10–12 inch step	10.0
WATER ACTIVITIES	
Canoeing, on camping trip	4.0
Canoeing, rowing, 2.0–6 mph, light to vigorous effort	3–12
Diving, springboard or platform	3.0
Kayaking	5.0
Paddle boating	4.0
Sailing, boat and board sailing, windsurfing, in general	3–5
Skiing, water	6.0
Skin-diving, fast, moderate, scuba diving	7–16
Snorkeling	5.0
Surfing, body or board	3.0
Swimming laps, freestyle, fast, vigorous effort	10.0
Swimming laps, freestyle, slow, moderate or light effort	7.0
Swimming laps, backstroke, general	7.0

Activity	METS
WATER ACTIVITIES—cont'd	
Swimming laps, breaststroke, general	10.0
Swimming, butterfly, general	11.0
Swimming, crawl, fast (75 yards/minute), vigorous effort	10.0
Swimming crawl, slow (50 yards/minute), moderate or light effort	7.0
Swimming, lake, ocean, river	6.0
Swimming, leisurely, not lap swimming, general	6.0
Swimming, sidestroke, general	8.0
Swimming, synchronized	8.0
Swimming, treading water, fast, vigorous	10.0
Swimming, treading water, moderate effort, general	4.0
Water aerobics, water calisthenics	4.0
Water polo	10.0
Water volleyball	3.0
Water jogging	8.0
WINTER ACTIVITIES	
Ice skating, general, 9 mph or less, rapidly (more than 9 mph)	5.5–9
Ski jumping	7.0
Skiing, general	7.0
Skiing, cross country 2.5 mph–8.0 mph	7–14
Skiing, downhill, light, moderate, vigorous	5–8
Sledding, tobogganing, bobsledding, luge	7.0
Snow shoeing	8.0
Snowmobiling	3.5
CONDITIONING EXERCISE	
Bicycling, stationary, general	7.0
Bicycling, stationary, (50–250 watts), very light—very vigorous	3–12.5
Calisthenics (eg., pushups, sit-ups, pull-ups, jumping jacks)	8.0
Calisthenics, home exercise, light or moderate effort (e.g., back exercises)	3.5
Circuit training, including some aerobic movement with general rest	8.0
Weight lifting (free weight, nautilus or universal type), power lifting or body building, vigorous effort	6.0
Stair—treadmill ergometer, general	9.0
Rowing, stationary, light to vigorous (50–200 watts)	3.5–12
Ski machine, general	7.0
Stretching, hatha yoga	2.5
Mild stretching	2.5
Teaching aerobic exercise class	6.0
Water aerobics, water calisthenics	4.0
BICYCLING	
Bicycling, BMX or mountain	8.5
Bicycling, <10 mph, leisure, to work or for pleasure	4.0
Bicycling, 10–11.9 mph, leisure, slow light effort	6.0
Bicycling, 12–13.9 mph, leisure, moderate effort	8.0
Bicycling, 14–15.9 mph, racing or leisure, fast, vigorous effort	10.0
Bicycling, 16–19 mph, racing very fast, racing general	12.0
Bicycling, >20 mph, racing, not drafting	16.0
WALKING/RUNNING	
Walking around house, strolling, shopping, leisure, walking dog	2.5–3.5
Walking 2.5 mph, firm surface	3.0
Walking 2.5 mph, downhill	2.8
Walking 3.0 mph, level firm surface	3.3
Walking 3.5 mph, level, firm surface	3.8
Walking 3.5 mph, uphill	6.0

Activity	METS
WALKING/RUNNING—cont'd	
Walking 4.0 mph, level, firm surface	5.0
Walking 4.5 mph, level, firm surface	6.3
Climbing hills with 0 to 9 pound load	7.0
Climbing hills with 10–20 pound load	7.5
Climbing hills with 21–42 pound load	8.0
Climbing hills with 42+ pound load	9.0
Going up stairs or climbing up a ladder	8.0
Race walking	6.5
Carrying infant or 15 pound load downstairs	3.5
Carrying 1–15 pound load upstairs	5.0
Carrying 16–24 pound load upstairs	6.0
Carrying 25–49 pound load upstairs	8.0
Carrying 50–74 pound load upstairs	10.0
Carrying 74+ pound load upstairs	12.0
Jog/walk combination (jogging component of less than 10 minutes)	6.0
Jogging, in general	7.0
Jogging, in place	8.0
Jogging on a mini-ramp	4.5
Running, 5 mph (12 min/mile)	8.0
Running, 5.2 mph (11.5 min/mile)	9.0
Running, 6 mph (10 min/mile)	10.0
Running, 6.7 mph (9 min/mile)	11.0
Running 7 mph (8.5 min/mile)	11.5
Running 7.5 mph (8 min/mile)	12.5
Running, 8 mph (7.5 min/mile)	13.5
Running 8.6 mph (7 min/mile)	14.0
Running 9 mph (6.5 min/mile)	15.0
Running 10 mph (6 min/mile)	16.0
Running 10.9 mph (5.5 min/mile)	18.0
Running, cross country	9.0
Running, stairs, up	15.0
Running, on a track, team practice	10.0
Running, training, pushing a wheelchair	8.0
SPORTS	
Archery	3.5
Badminton, social singles and doubles, general	4.5–7
Basketball, game, non-game, general	6–8
Basketball	4.5
Basketball, wheelchair	6.5
Billiards	2.5
Bowling	3.0
Boxing, punching bag	6.0
Boxing, sparring	9.0
Children's games (hopscotch, 4-square, dodge ball, playground, etc.)	5.0
Coaching: football, soccer, basketball, baseball, swimming, etc.	4.0
Fencing	6.0
Football, competitive	9.0
Football, touch, flag, general	8.0
Football or baseball, playing catch	2.5
Frisbee playing, general	3.0
Frisbee, ultimate	8.0
Golf, walking and carrying clubs	4.5

Activity	METS
SPORTS—cont'd	
Golf, miniature, driving range	3.0
Golf, walking and pulling clubs	4.3
Golf, using power cart	3.5
Handball, general, team	8–12
Hockey, field or ice	8.0
Horseback riding, walking to trotting	2.5–6.5
Horseshoe pitching	3.0
Judo, jujitsu, karate, kick boxing, tae kwon do	10.0
Kickball	7.0
Lacrosse	8.0
Orienteering	9.0
Paddleball, competitive, casual, general	6–10
Polo	8.0
Racquetball	7–10
Rock climbing	11.0
Rock climbing, rappelling	8.0
Rope jumping (varying intensity and speed)	7–10
Rugby	10
Shuffleboard, bocce ball, lawn bowling	3.0
Skating, roller	7.0
Roller blading (in-line skating)	12.5
Sky diving	3.5
Soccer, casual-competitive	7–10
Softball or baseball, fast or slow pitch, general	5.0
Softball, officiating	4.0
Softball, pitching	6.0
Squash	12.0
Table tennis, ping pong	4.0
Tai chi	4.0
Tennis, doubles to singles	5–8
Trampoline	3.5
Volleyball	3–8

Medicine and Science in Sports and Exercise. (supplement) 32 (9), 2000.

Determining Your Weekly Estimated Energy Expenditure (EEE)

Record your activities for each day with its corresponding MET value found on pages in Appendix C.

	Monday	Tuesday	Wednesday	Thursday	Friday	Saturday	Sunday
5:00 am							
6:00 am							
7:00 am							
8:00 am							
9:00 am							
10:00 am							
11:00 am							
12:00 pm							
1:00 pm							
2:00 pm							
3:00 pm							
4:00 pm							
5:00 pm							
6:00 pm							
7:00 pm							
8:00 pm							
9:00 pm							
10:00 pm							
11:00 pm							
12:00 am							
1:00 am							
2:00 am							
3:00 am							
4:00 am							

Fill in the number of hours spent doing activities in the following MET value ranges for each day.

Level of Activity	MET value	Monday		Tuesday		Wednesday		Thursday		Friday		Saturday		Sunday	
# hrs × MET value		# hrs	×MET value	# hrs	×MET value	# hrs	×MET value	# hrs	×MET value	# hrs	×MET value	# hrs	×MET value	# hrs	×MET value
Resting	1.0														
Light	1.1–2.9														
Moderate	3.0–6.0														
Hard	6.1 +														
Sum Totals															
Total × weight (kg) =															

Determining Daily Energy Needs

Step 1: The Harris-Benedict Equation

- Men: BMR = 66 + (6.2 × wt in lbs ___) + (12.7 × ht in inches ___) − (6.8 × age in years ___)
- Women: BMR = 665 + (4.4 × wt in lbs ___) + (4.3 × ht in inches ___) − (4.7 × age in years ___)

Your BMR = _____

Step 2: Determine Total Daily Energy Needs by multiplying the BMR from Step 1 by the appropriate activity factor from the chart below.

Activity Factors:

- Sedentary (little or no exercise) =   BMR × 1.2
- Lightly active (light exercise/sports 1–3 days/week) =   BMR × 1.4
- Moderately active (moderate exercise/sports 3–5 days/week) =   BMR × 1.6
- Very active (hard exercise/sports 6–7 days/week) =   BMR × 1.7
- Extremely active (hard exercise/sports and physical job OR 2X a day training) = BMR × 1.9

The formula used above gives the energy needs for *maintaining weight* at the current activity level.

Your daily caloric needs = _____

Step 3: (Optional) Factor for Weight Loss or Gain

- Subtract 250–500 calories a day for wt. loss of ∼ ½ to 1 lb. per week.
- Add 250–500 calories a day for wt. gain of ∼ ½ to 1 lb. per week.

Your daily caloric needs adjusted for weight loss or gain = _____

*There are 3,500 calories in a pound of stored body fat. Creating a 3,500-calorie deficit in a week through diet and exercise will cause a loss of one pound during that week. It is **not** advisable to drop calorie levels below 1,200 calories per day for women or 1,800 per day for men.*

Step 4: How many grams of carbohydrates?

_____ calories/day × 0.6 = _____ calories from carbohydrates (CHO)

_____ calories from CHO ÷ 4 calories/gram = _____ grams of CHO

Step 5: How many grams of protein?

Sedentary Populations	Protein Intake (g/kg/day)	Athletic Populations	Protein Intake (g/kg/day)
Children	1.0	Recreational athletes (4–5x/wk for 30 min)	0.8–1.0
Adolescents	1.0–1.5	Endurance training athletes: moderate to extreme volume	1.2–1.6
Adults	0.8–1.0	Resistance training athletes:	1.2–1.7
		Novice	1.5–1.7
		Steady state	1.0–1.2
Pregnant women	+6–10 g/day	Adolescent athletes during growth spurt	1.5
Breastfeeding women	+12–16 g/day		

Source: Maughan, R.J. and L.M. Burke. 2002. Sports Nutrition. Blackwell Publishing. pg. 30.

Based on the table above, determine your appropriate protein needs by multiplying your body weight in kg by the protein factor.

Body weight in pounds = _____ lb ÷ 2.2 kg = _____ kg body weight

Protein needs = _____ g/kg/day (protein factor) × _____ kg body weight = _____ g of protein

Step 6: How many grams of fat?

_____ calories/day × 0.3 = _____ calories from fat

_____ calories from fat ÷ 9 = _____ g of fat

Logs

Activity Log

Name _____   Class/Day/Hour _____

Date	Time AM/PM	Activity	Duration (Min) and/or Distance (Laps/Miles)	Calories Expended	HR/RPE	Comments: How did you feel? tired, sick, good

Activity Log

Name _____   Class/Day/Hour _____

Date	Time AM/PM	Activity	Duration (Min) and/or Distance (Laps/Miles)	Calories Expended	HR/RPE	Comments: How did you feel? tired, sick, good

Activity Log

Name _____   Class/Day/Hour _____

Date	Time AM/PM	Activity	Duration (Min) and/or Distance (Laps/Miles)	Calories Expended	HR/RPE	Comments: How did you feel? tired, sick, good

Activity Log

Name _____   Class/Day/Hour _____

Date	Time AM/PM	Activity	Duration (Min) and/or Distance (Laps/Miles)	Calories Expended	HR/RPE	Comments: How did you feel? tired, sick, good

Weight Training Log

Date																
Exercises	S e t s	Wt	Reps	Wt	Reps	Wt	Reps	Wt	Reps	Wt	Reps	Wt	Reps	Wt	Reps	Wt	Reps
	1																
	2																
	3																
	1																
	2																
	3																
	1																
	2																
	3																
	1																
	2																
	3																
	1																
	2																
	3																
	1																
	2																
	3																
	1																
	2																
	3																
	1																
	2																
	3																
	1																
	2																
	3																
	1																
	2																
	3																
	1																
	2																
	3																
	1																
	2																
	3																

Weight Training Log

Date																
Exercises	Sets	Wt	Reps	Wt	Reps	Wt	Reps	Wt	Reps	Wt	Reps	Wt	Reps	Wt	Reps	Wt	Reps
	1																
	2																
	3																
	1																
	2																
	3																
	1																
	2																
	3																
	1																
	2																
	3																
	1																
	2																
	3																
	1																
	2																
	3																
	1																
	2																
	3																
	1																
	2																
	3																
	1																
	2																
	3																
	1																
	2																
	3																
	1																
	2																
	3																
	1																
	2																
	3																
	1																
	2																
	3																

Weight Training Log

Date		Wt	Reps	Wt	Reps	Wt	Reps	Wt	Reps	Wt	Reps	Wt	Reps	Wt	Reps	Wt	Reps
Exercises	Sets	Wt	Reps	Wt	Reps	Wt	Reps	Wt	Reps	Wt	Reps	Wt	Reps	Wt	Reps	Wt	Reps
	1																
	2																
	3																
	1																
	2																
	3																
	1																
	2																
	3																
	1																
	2																
	3																
	1																
	2																
	3																
	1																
	2																
	3																
	1																
	2																
	3																
	1																
	2																
	3																
	1																
	2																
	3																
	1																
	2																
	3																
	1																
	2																
	3																
	1																
	2																
	3																

Weight Training Log

Date			Wt	Reps	Wt	Reps	Wt	Reps	Wt	Reps	Wt	Reps	Wt	Reps	Wt	Reps	Wt	Reps
Exercises	Sets		Wt	Reps	Wt	Reps	Wt	Reps	Wt	Reps	Wt	Reps	Wt	Reps	Wt	Reps	Wt	Reps
	1																	
	2																	
	3																	
	1																	
	2																	
	3																	
	1																	
	2																	
	3																	
	1																	
	2																	
	3																	
	1																	
	2																	
	3																	
	1																	
	2																	
	3																	
	1																	
	2																	
	3																	
	1																	
	2																	
	3																	
	1																	
	2																	
	3																	
	1																	
	2																	
	3																	
	1																	
	2																	
	3																	
	1																	
	2																	
	3																	
	1																	
	2																	
	3																	

Daily Nutrition Log

Date _____   Day _____

	FOOD	PORTION SIZE
Breakfast—Time: _____ Location: _____ What influenced your food choice? _____ _____ _____ Time spent eating: _____		
Lunch—Time: _____ Location: _____ What influenced your food choice? _____ _____ _____ Time spent eating: _____		
Dinner—Time: _____ Location: _____ What influenced your food choice? _____ _____ _____ Time spent eating: _____		
Snacks: Time of day _____ What influenced your snack choices? _____ _____ Fluid intake: Water: _____ cups/oz Alcohol: _____ Soda Pop: _____ Other: _____		

Evaluate your food intake:

- Carbohydrates: How many servings?
  How many servings of whole grains?
- Fruits & Vegetables: How many servings?
  How many were bright red, orange, or dark green?
- Milk: How many servings?
  How many were low-fat options?
- Meat/Beans: How many servings?
  How many from lean choices?

Daily Nutrition Log

Date _____   Day _____

	FOOD	PORTION SIZE
Breakfast—Time: _____ Location: _____ What influenced your food choice? _____ _____ _____ Time spent eating: _____		
Lunch—Time: _____ Location: _____ What influenced your food choice? _____ _____ _____ Time spent eating: _____		
Dinner—Time: _____ Location: _____ What influenced your food choice? _____ _____ _____ Time spent eating: _____		
Snacks: Time of day _____ What influenced your snack choices? _____ _____ Fluid intake: Water: _____ cups/oz Alcohol: _____ Soda Pop: _____ Other: _____		

Evaluate your food intake:

- Carbohydrates: How many servings?
  How many servings of whole grains?
- Fruits & Vegetables: How many servings?
  How many were bright red, orange, or dark green?
- Milk: How many servings?
  How many were low-fat options?
- Meat/Beans: How many servings?
  How many from lean choices?

Daily Nutrition Log

Date _____   Day _____

	FOOD	PORTION SIZE
Breakfast—Time: _____ Location: _____ What influenced your food choice? _____ _____ _____ Time spent eating: _____		
Lunch—Time: _____ Location: _____ What influenced your food choice? _____ _____ _____ Time spent eating: _____		
Dinner—Time: _____ Location: _____ What influenced your food choice? _____ _____ _____ Time spent eating: _____		
Snacks: Time of day _____ What influenced your snack choices? _____ _____ Fluid intake: Water: _____ cups/oz Alcohol: _____ Soda Pop: _____ Other: _____		

Evaluate your food intake:

- Carbohydrates: How many servings?
  How many servings of whole grains?
- Fruits & Vegetables: How many servings?
  How many were bright red, orange, or dark green?
- Milk: How many servings?
  How many were low-fat options?
- Meat/Beans: How many servings?
  How many from lean choices?

Daily Nutrition Log

Date _____   Day _____

	FOOD	PORTION SIZE
Breakfast—Time: _____ Location: _____ What influenced your food choice? _____ _____ _____ Time spent eating: _____		
Lunch—Time: _____ Location: _____ What influenced your food choice? _____ _____ _____ Time spent eating: _____		
Dinner—Time: _____ Location: _____ What influenced your food choice? _____ _____ _____ Time spent eating: _____		
Snacks: Time of day _____ What influenced your snack choices? _____ _____ Fluid intake: Water: _____ cups/oz Alcohol: _____ Soda Pop: _____ Other: _____		

Evaluate your food intake:

- Carbohydrates: How many servings?
  How many servings of whole grains?
- Fruits & Vegetables: How many servings?
  How many were bright red, orange, or dark green?
- Milk: How many servings?
  How many were low-fat options?
- Meat/Beans: How many servings?
  How many from lean choices?

Daily Nutrition Log

Date _____   Day _____

	FOOD	PORTION SIZE
Breakfast—Time: _____ Location: _____ What influenced your food choice? _____ _____ _____ Time spent eating: _____		
Lunch—Time: _____ Location: _____ What influenced your food choice? _____ _____ _____ Time spent eating: _____		
Dinner—Time: _____ Location: _____ What influenced your food choice? _____ _____ _____ Time spent eating: _____		
Snacks: Time of day _____ What influenced your snack choices? _____ _____ Fluid intake: Water: _____ cups/oz Alcohol: _____ Soda Pop: _____ Other: _____		

Evaluate your food intake:

- Carbohydrates: How many servings?
  How many servings of whole grains?
- Fruits & Vegetables: How many servings?
  How many were bright red, orange, or dark green?
- Milk: How many servings?
  How many were low-fat options?
- Meat/Beans: How many servings?
  How many from lean choices?

Daily Nutrition Log

Date _____ Day _____

	FOOD	PORTION SIZE
Breakfast—Time: _____ Location: _____ What influenced your food choice? _____ _____ _____ Time spent eating: _____		
Lunch—Time: _____ Location: _____ What influenced your food choice? _____ _____ _____ Time spent eating: _____		
Dinner—Time: _____ Location: _____ What influenced your food choice? _____ _____ _____ Time spent eating: _____		
Snacks: Time of day _____ What influenced your snack choices? _____ _____		
Fluid intake: Water: _____ cups/oz Alcohol: _____ Soda Pop: _____ Other: _____		

Evaluate your food intake:

- Carbohydrates: How many servings?
  How many servings of whole grains?
- Fruits & Vegetables: How many servings?
  How many were bright red, orange, or dark green?
- Milk: How many servings?
  How many were low-fat options?
- Meat/Beans: How many servings?
  How many from lean choices?

Daily Nutrition Log

Date _____   Day _____

	FOOD	PORTION SIZE
Breakfast—Time: _____ Location: _____ What influenced your food choice? _____ _____ _____ Time spent eating: _____		
Lunch—Time: _____ Location: _____ What influenced your food choice? _____ _____ _____ Time spent eating: _____		
Dinner—Time: _____ Location: _____ What influenced your food choice? _____ _____ _____ Time spent eating: _____		
Snacks: Time of day _____ What influenced your snack choices? _____ _____ Fluid intake: Water: _____ cups/oz Alcohol: _____ Soda Pop: _____ Other: _____		

Evaluate your food intake:

- Carbohydrates: How many servings?
  How many servings of whole grains?
- Fruits & Vegetables: How many servings?
  How many were bright red, orange, or dark green?
- Milk: How many servings?
  How many were low-fat options?
- Meat/Beans: How many servings?
  How many from lean choices?